SIMPLY ELEGANT

MORE TECHNIQUES IN CAKE DESIGN

GERALDINE RANDLESOME

LESOME PRESS

ACKNOWLEDGEMENTS

Geraldine Randlesome would like to thank: Janet Foster for the lovely techniques (shown on page 80) for the colour flow bride and groom; Estelle Pilissof for the idea of the filigree pattern (shown on page 77); Colleen Willis for a very similar idea (shown on the cake on page 28); and finally, Frank Rae of Forget-Me-Not flower shop in Oakville, Ontario, for his wonderful arrangements of the gum paste flowers (see pages 6 and 73).

All supplies for the cakes—Bekenal tips, Renshaw sugar paste (fondant/regal ice), gum paste cutters—supplied by Creative Cutters, 3 Tannery Court, Richmond Hill, Ontario, Canada, L4C 7V5.

PUBLISHED IN 1988 BY LESOME PRESS
             3 Tannery Court
             Richmond Hill
             Ontario, Canada, L4C 7V5

ISBN 0-9692523-1

Design and Production: Fortunato Aglialoro and Linda Pellowe, Falcom Design and Communications Inc.

Photography: Gadi Hoz. Photographics, Inc.   Gadi Hoz/Amir Gavriely

Line Illustrations: Lily Con

Editing: Caroline Stephens

Typing and Typesetting: Patty Sandquist and Attic Typesetting Inc.

Colour Separations, Printing and Binding: Friesen Printers (D.W. Friesen & Sons Ltd.), Altona, Manitoba

Printed in Canada

Foreword

In the art of sugar work it is always exciting to welcome a new book by a talented exponent of the craft.

I consider it a privilege to write the foreword for Geraldine Randlesome's third book, *Simply Elegant*, on skills and techniques in the field. This artist has issued challenges throughout the world for cake decorators to follow: her skills in Oriental stringwork, floating collars, extension borders, design and moulded flowers have already won her major awards in many countries.

Through our mutual love of this craft we formed a friendship which was further developed when we met in Zimbabwe where we conducted classes and gave demonstrations. At that time I was able to see and appreciate her talents as she performed intricate techniques with perfection.

I am sure all decorators will enjoy the challenges offered throughout this book as I have, and share my admiration for its author.

Bernice J. Vercoe.

Bernice J. Vercoe
Sydney, Australia, 1988

Contents

Introduction

In December 1984, when I was asked to create a wedding cake using the highly unusual colour combination of black, white and silver, my first reaction was "not black for a wedding cake!" But when I began to think about what it could be like, my creative juices really began to flow.

The cake I ultimately designed created a sensation. Technically, it had been very difficult, but its simple beauty made the effort more than worthwhile.

My next attempt with black and white (shown on page 61 of this book) was seen in London, the United States and Japan. Wherever we went, this elegant black and white cake inspired awe, amazement and wonder. Everyone's excitement and appreciation so moved me that I was inspired to write a book featuring only black and white cakes. I began this book in October, 1986 and it has been a long time in the making. Since then, I have expanded my original idea to include a full range of unusual designs in a variety of colours. All the cakes, gum paste flowers and edible cake tops pictured in this book are my own original designs and creations.

My last book, *Techniques in Cake Design*, contained my floating collar techniques. It was so advanced in many respects that I decided this time to write a simpler, yet inspiring book. I hope you will be as excited about it as I am. If it sparks your interest and challenges you to reach new heights of creativity and skill, then I will consider it a success.

Geraldine

Geraldine Randlesome
Toronto 1988

Chapter 1

Flowers and the Art of Cake Decorating

Step-by-Step Arrangements for Two Cakes

What can be more exquisite on a cake top than a display of lovely flowers? Gum paste or fresh, nothing compares to their perfect beauty. Truly a universal delight, flowers everywhere are associated with beauty and joy.

Flower arranging as an art goes back many thousands of years. It was popular in Ancient Egypt and, in Ancient Greece and Rome, flowers were used in head garlands. In Medieval Europe and Britain, flower arranging as we know it today became very popular.

I realized early on that cake decorating and flower arranging go hand in hand: the flowers used to embellish a cake must match the colour and style of the cake itself and also the occasion for which the cake is made. The flowers on a wedding cake, for example, must not only be beautiful (after all, what occasion is planned with more care or enthusiasm) but they must compliment the bride, her dress and bouquet, the dresses and bouquets of her attendants and the floral arrangements used to decorate the tables.

My own love of flowers and floral arrangements led me to perfect the art, by reading many books on the subject, taking classes and practising for hours. It is no accident, therefore, that the first letters of the chapter headings of this book spell the word "flowers"—Filigree, Lace, Other Techniques, Wedding Cakes, Elegance, Ruffles and Show Cakes.

I strongly recommend that anyone seriously interested in the art of cake decorating take classes in flower arranging. But first, to help you on your way, here are step-by-step instructions for assembling the flowers for 2 of the cakes in this book.

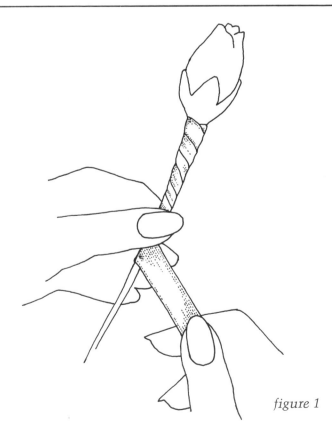

figure 1

Victorian Posy Ruffle Cake Flowers

Prepare the roses by taping a small amount of dried babies' breath to every flower. (This acts as a cushion to the flowers and helps to prevent breakage.) Tape your main rosebuds with the peach ribbon as shown in the large posy. *See figure 1.* With a hot glue gun, glue the ribbon and attach it to the end of the stem.

Arrange the flowers by starting with the buds then adding the roses and open blown-silk leaves, butterflies and bunches of pearls. Place the ribbon bows at the end of the flowers, then place inside the posy holder.

To Make the Posy Holder

Take a straight piece of lace and run a very thin wire through the top of the lace. *See figure 2.* Gather the lace to form a circle. *See figure 3.* Place the flowers inside the posy holder adjusting the sizes as required. Make large satin bows and, with the glue gun, attach them to the posy holder.

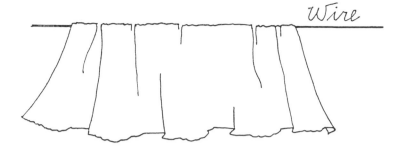

figure 2

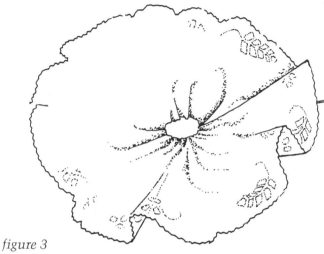

figure 3

White Classic Wedding Cake Flowers

Tape together with florist tape one stephanotis and 2 ivy leaves. Then, using more florist tape, add another stephanotis, pearls and 2 more ivy leaves. Add to this a rosebud, 2 ivy leaves, then pearls. Next, attach a semi-open rose and a stephanotis, then pearls and ivy leaves. Add another semi-open rose, more ivy leaves, then 3 open roses and ivy leaves. Finally, attach orchids and more ivy leaves. Make 3 bows of ribbon and tape to the top of the arrangement. *See figure 4.*

figure 4

Chapter 2

Filigree pattern

Filigree

A very delicate look to enhance any cake.

This lace work originated in South Africa. Fine lace pieces are made off the cake and are placed on it when dry.

Bar Mitzvah Cake

Single Tier Hexagon

Step 1. Cover the board with fondant following instructions on page 91 and let dry overnight. Cover the cake with fondant and place on the board. With a #2 tip, pipe a small bead border around the base of the cake. Let dry for at least 1 hour.

Step 2. Tape the pattern over a soft drink can or glass—then place a sheet of cooking film over the pattern. *See figure 1.* With a #0 tip, pipe the filigree pattern and allow it to dry at least 30 minutes before placing it on a sheet of foam. *See figure 2.* Make an extra 3 pieces to allow for breakage.

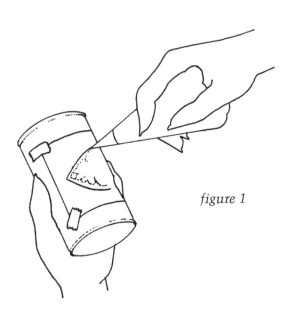

figure 1

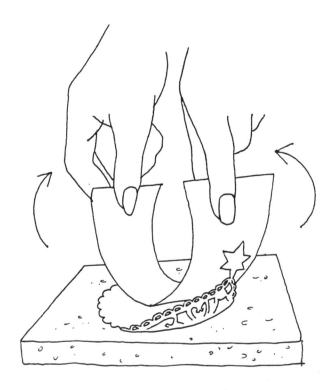

figure 2

VICTORIAN POSY RUFFLE CAKE FLOWERS

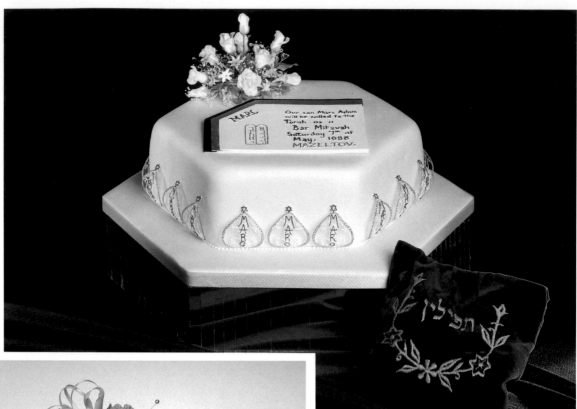

Our son Marc Adam
will be called to the
Torah as a
Bar Mitzvah
Saturday 7th of
May, 1988
MAZELTOV.

BAR MITZVAH CAKE

WHITE CLASSIC WEDDING CAKE FLOWERS

GOLD EDGE FILIGREE CAKE

CHOCOLATE ECSTASY CAKE

BLUE ORIENTAL CAKE

SHELL CAKE

Step 3. With a #0 tip, pipe 3 dots of icing on the reverse side of the pattern. *See figure 3.* Then, very gently place the pieces on the cake. *See figure 4.*

Step 4. (optional) A very personal touch is to add the child's name to your design. To paint the Star of David and the child's name, use a mixture of royal blue food powder and white alcohol. Paint the sides of the filigree pieces with silver colour.

Embellishments

White roses

Blue and white hyacinths

Pastillage sugar card in the form of the invitation card (For instructions on how to prepare pastillage, see page 90)

Filigree (See pattern illustration)

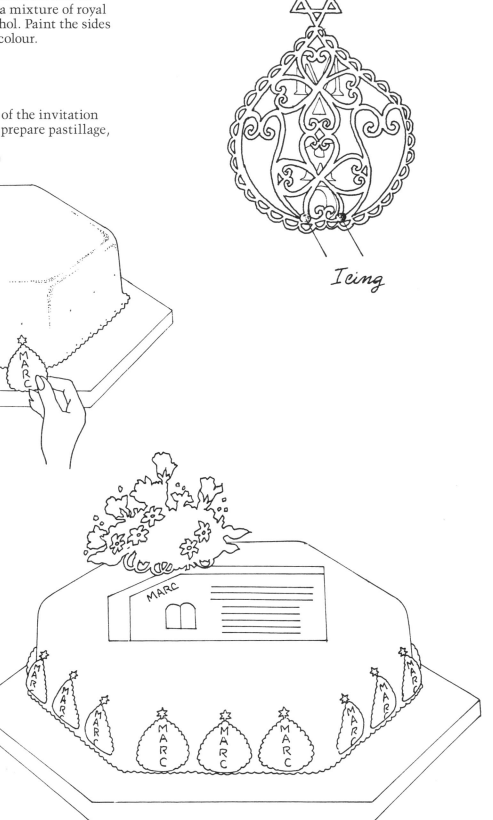

figure 3

Icing

Icing

figure 4

Filigree pattern

Gold Edge Filigree Cake

Single Tier Round

Many children are asked to help in fund-raising projects. When my daughter asked for a cake for her school, I combined her school colours and her school badge to decorate the cake.

Step 1. Cover the board with fondant following instructions on page 91 and let dry overnight. Cover the cake with fondant and place on the board. With a #2 tip, pipe a small bead border around the base of the cake and let dry at least 1 hour.

Step 2. Make a false collar and place it around the cake. Remove the collar and keep folding it in half until the desired filigree pattern is reached, (remembering to allow ¼″ (5 mm) of space).

Step 3. Tape the pattern over a glass or soft drink can. *See figure 1*, and cover with a sheet of cooking film. Then, with a #0 tip, pipe the filigree pieces. Let dry at least 30 minutes.

Step 4. Roll out very thin a tiny piece of gum paste. Cut out 2 small blossoms for each filigree pattern. Place the blossoms on a small piece of foam or sponge and, with a small-ended metal ball tool, cup the petals towards the centre of the flower. *See figure 2.*

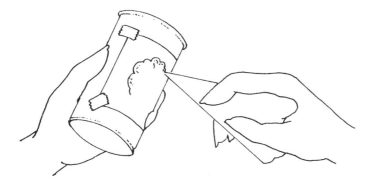

figure 1

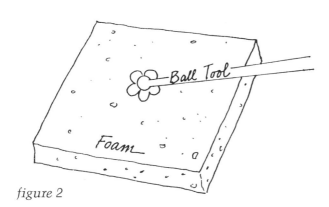

figure 2

figure 3

With royal icing, attach the blossoms to the centre of the heart. *See figure 3.* Continue piping the filigree pieces allowing 3-4 extra pieces for breakage.

Step 5. Attach the filigree pieces to the cake, *See figure 4*, painting the sides with a non-toxic gold colour. Let dry.

Embellishments

Mini tiger lilies
Leaves
Dried babies' breath
Ribbon
Personal design such as colour flow crest or badge
Filigree (See pattern illustration)

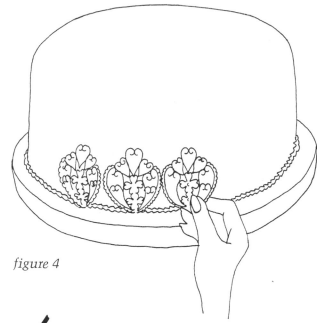

figure 4

figure 1

Chocolate Ecstasy Cake

Single Tier Round

Chocolate and carrot cake lovers will really go wild over this new creation featuring Chocolate Chip Carrot Cake with Chocolate Fondant icing.

Step 1. Cover the board with chocolate fondant (recipe on page 90) and let dry overnight. Cover the cake (see page 92) with chocolate fondant and place on the board. With a #2 tip, pipe a small bead border around the base of the cake. Let dry at least 24 hours. In the meantime, pipe the large filigree pieces.

Step 2. Make a false collar and divide. Then make the filigree pattern to match the false collar divisions. *See figure 1.*

Step 3. Place the pattern on a piece of plexiglass approximately 9″ square. Cover the pattern with cooking film or thin plastic. *See figure 2.* Then, with a #0 tip, pipe the filigree pieces, allowing a few extra pieces for breakage.

Step 4. Place 2 rows of ribbon around the cake. With a #0 tip and *very* small bead border, attach the filigree pieces. As you attach each piece, very gently pull the piece away from the cake. *See figure 3.* Continue until all the filigree pieces are on the cake. Let dry at least 1 hour.

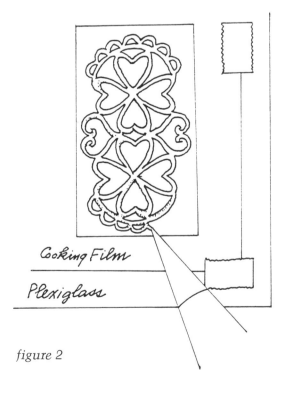

Cooking Film

Plexiglass

figure 2

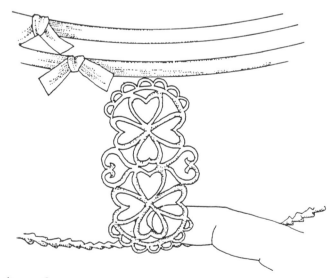

figure 3

Step 5. With a #0 tip, pipe a scallop to join all the pieces together. *See figure 4.*

Step 6. Make very small forget-me-nots by placing on a small piece of foam and rotating the ball tool around. Pipe embroidery, then attach small flowers.

Embellishments

Gum paste roses combined with dried babies' breath
Embroidery (See pattern illustration)
Candy dish
Pastillage
White truffles such as Champagne Wedding Truffles
(Recipe page 89) or Apricot truffles

figure 4

Embroidery pattern

Chapter 3

Lace

The ultimate in cake decorating—fine lace pieces combined with Australian lace work. An exquisite creation to challenge the decorator and answer every bride's dreams.

figure 1

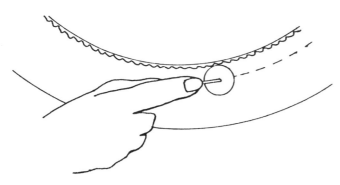

Blue Oriental Cake

Single Tier Round

When I was first asked to create a cake in an oriental style using the colours red, gold, blue and white with a hint of black, I considered it quite a challenge. This combination of colours is traditional in the Orient and I began to think of how to combine them in a cake design. For the top of the cake, I used a stencil of the famous 'Willow' china pattern. For the sides, I was inspired to create a string design resembling the undulating movement of the dragon's body in Chinese ceremonial processions. From there, it naturally followed to place the dragon's heads on top of the cake.

Step 1. Cover the board with fondant following instructions on page 91 and let dry overnight. Cover the cake with fondant, place the cake on the board and, with a #2 tip, pipe a small bead border around the base of the cake. Let dry.

Step 2. Make a batch of pastillage (recipe on page 90) and roll out to cut an 8″ circle. Let dry overnight.

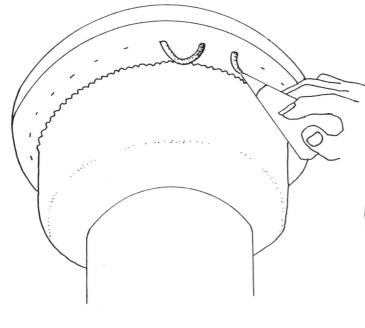

figure 2

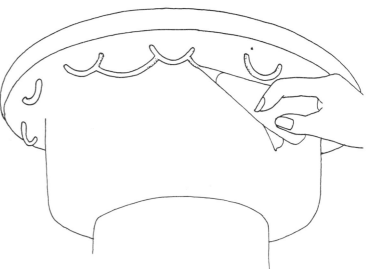

figure 3

Step 3. Make a false collar, cutting out the design of the top pattern. Place the collar on the cake and, with a pin or dressmaker's wheel, mark the pattern on the sides of the cake. Remove the collar and mark the pattern on the boards. (This can be done by placing a round disk or button on the board and, with a pin, marking both sides of the disk. *See figure 1.*)

Step 4. Turn both the board and the cake upside down onto a smaller 6″ (15 cm) styro dummy to elevate. With a #2 tip, pipe scallops from mark to mark. *See figures 2 and 3.* Let dry 4-6 hours or overnight. Turn the cake right side up and, with a #2 tip, pipe a scallop in every other scallop. *See figure 4.* Let dry overnight.

Step 5. With a #0 tip, pipe the crossover strings in the oval open bridge. *See figure 5.* Let dry. With a #0 tip, pipe the strings from the pattern on the side of the cake to the bridge. (Extreme care must be taken not to break the bridges when piping this design.) *See figure 6.* Let dry.

Step 6. With a #0 tip, pipe the small scallops around the top and base of the strings. *See figure 7.* Let dry.

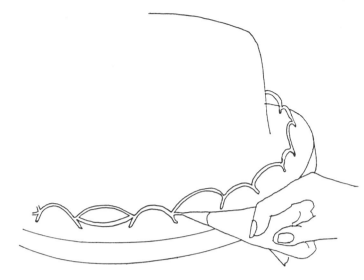

figure 4

figure 5

figure 6

figure 7

Step 7. Mold the dragons' heads and side design from gum paste or pastillage. Let dry. With a #0 tip, pipe the good luck embroidery pattern onto the sides of the cake.

Step 8. Sand the edge of the pastillage circle. *Very* gently, place the willow pattern stencil onto the circle and, with a long palette knife, spread royal icing over the stencil. Clean the knife and pull it across the stencil to remove the excess icing. Then, very gently, remove the pattern.

Step 9. With a #2 tip, attach the pattern to the centre of the top of the cake and pipe around using a small bead border. Attach the dragon heads to the cake with royal icing and repeat for the side patterns. Paint the pieces using white alcohol and food colours using gold colour to highlight the side pieces. Let dry. To finish, either place ribbon or attach mosaic tiles around the board.

Embellishments
Embroidery (See pattern illustration)
Willow stencil (See pattern illustration)

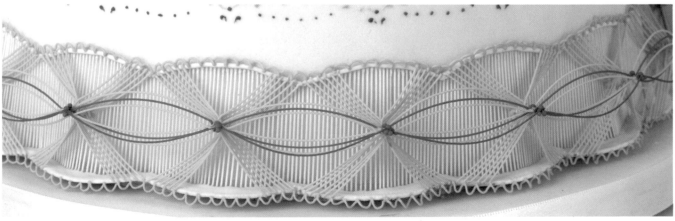

CONGRATULATIONS CAKE

SPORTING DAYS CAKE

HARLEQUIN CAKE

BLACK CLASSIC CAKE

SUGAR MUSIC BOX

Embroidery pattern

Willow Stencil

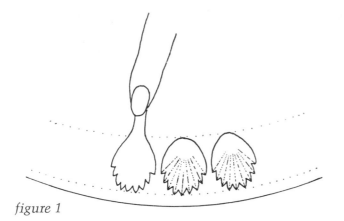

figure 1

Shell Cake

Single Tier Round

String work is a very beautiful enhancement for cakes, but I have always questioned why the strings have traditionally been applied vertically. There is really no reason to limit yourself to a vertical pattern of string work. There are, in fact, many ways to decorate using this technique. Why not break with tradition and try something totally different?

For this cake, I took my idea from the sugar shell on top and carried the design through onto the stringwork shells on the sides of the cake.

Step 1. Cover the board with fondant and, while the fondant is still wet, press a shell design around the edges of the board. *See figure 1.* Let dry overnight. Cover the cake with fondant and place on the board. With a #2 tip, pipe a small bead border around the base of the cake. Let dry at least 1 hour.

Step 2. Mark the outline of the shell on the side of the cake. *See figure 2.* With a #1 tip and royal icing, pipe the marked outline with 2 rows of icing. Let dry.

Step 3. From the high point of the shell, pipe the strings from the top to the base. *See figure 3.* With the cake raised on the side, continue piping the side strings. (Piping the strings on either side of the shell can be made easier by placing a book or cloth under the cake to help the strings fall straight. *See figure 4.*) When one side is complete, raise the other side of the cake and continue piping. Let dry.

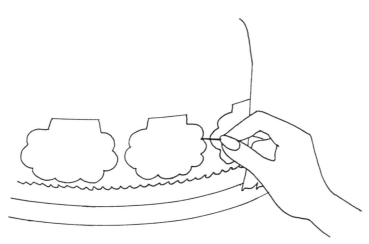

figure 2

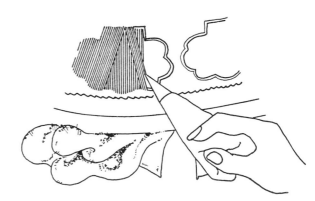

figure 4

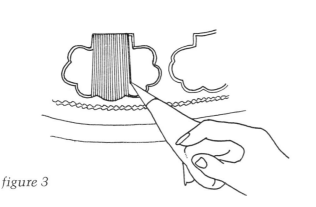

figure 3

Step 4. With a #0 tip, pipe a small scallop around the top of the cake. Pipe a small dot on each join. *See figure 5.* Attach ribbon around the cake board.

Embellishments

Sugar shell with roses
Small calla lily
Hyacinth
Silk leaves
Pearls

To make sugar shell:

Step 1. Dust both halves of the shell mold with cornstarch. Roll out pastillage on cornstarch quite thinly. Press into the shell mold, trimming the edges of the mold. *See figure 6.* Gently release the mold so that it is free to turn out when dry. Leave overnight to dry.

Step 2. When dry, sand the edges with a fine sandpaper. Fill the base with florist oasis. Pipe a small amount of royal icing into the empty shell so that the oasis will stick. *See figure 7.*

Step 3. Arrange flowers in the shell starting with the leaves, then the filler flowers and lastly, the main flowers and pearls.

Step 4. Attach the lid with royal icing, propping the lid up against a tall glass jar to hold until the lid is dry. Place on top of the cake with pearls.

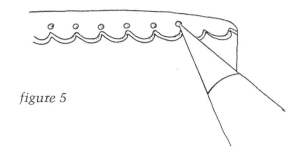

figure 5

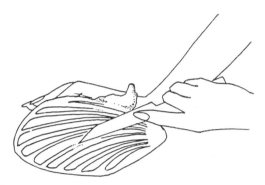

figure 6

figure 7

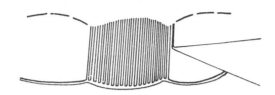

figure 1

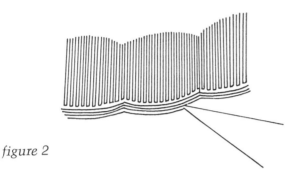

figure 2

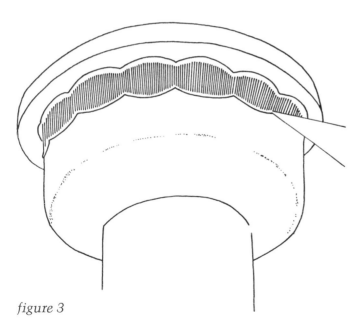

figure 3

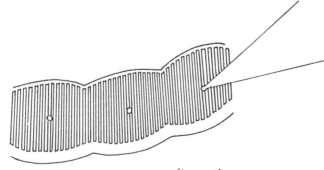

figure 4

Congratulations Cake

Single Tier Round

A cake to challenge even the most advanced decorator.

Step 1. Cover the board with fondant following instructions on page 91 and leave overnight to dry. Cover the cake with fondant and place on the board. With a #2 tip, pipe a small bead border around the base of the cake. Let dry.

Step 2. Make a false collar and place around the cake. Mark the design on the side of the cake, then remove the collar. With a #2 tip, pipe the bridge lines following instructions on page 92. Let dry. Flood in the bridge work. Let dry.

Step 3. With a #0 tip, pipe the strings from the top line to the bridge work. *See figure 1.* Continue all the way around the cake. Let dry. Repeat the bridging for 4 rows. *See figure 2.* Let dry. Flood in. Let dry.

Step 4. Very carefully, turn the cake upside down and stand it on a large tin or glass jar. With a #2 tip, pipe one bridge line only over the top of the strings. *See figure 3.* Let dry. Remove cake and place on turntable. With a #2 tip, pipe one dot in the centre of the strings. *See figure 4.* Let dry.

Step 5. With a #0 tip, pipe the strings from the top left hand corner down and around the dot. *See figure 5.* Repeat, only this time pipe from the right hand down. Repeat from the lower left hand up to the centre. Repeat for the right hand. Repeat whole sequence above until 5 rows have been completed. Let dry.

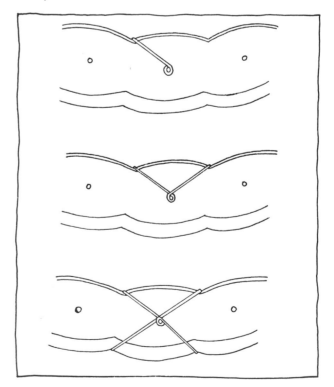

figure 5

Step 6. With a #0 tip, and the lighter shade of royal icing, pipe a scallop from the centre dot to the next centre dot. *See figure 6*. Let dry. When dry, very carefully turn the cake upside down and stand the cake on a large (48 oz) tin or glass jar. Pipe the scallop to match the other scallop. *See figure 7*. Let dry. Remove cake from tin or jar and restore to an upright position. Repeat the last 2 steps using the darker shade of royal icing. Repeat once more using the lighter shade. Let dry.

Step 7. The final scallop extends from the cake and can be piped by either holding the cake against a wall, *See figure 8*, or tipping cake up using a tilt turntable. Pipe the last row. Let dry.

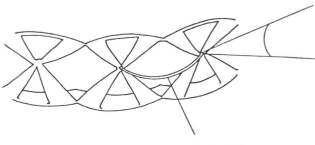

figure 6　　　First Scallop

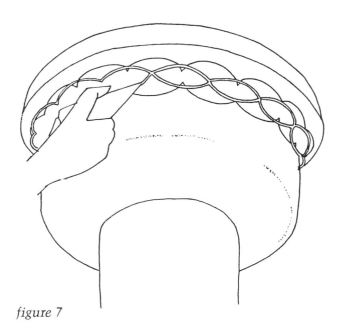

figure 7

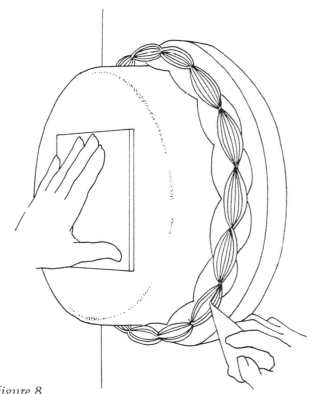

figure 8

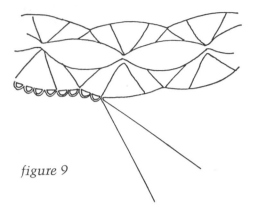

figure 9

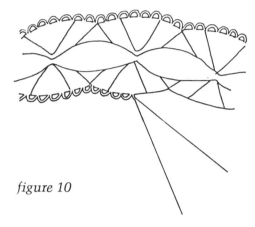

figure 10

Step 8. With a #0 tip, pipe a small scallop around the base of the cake. *See figure 9.* Very gently, turn the cake upside down following the instructions in Step 4 and pipe the top scallop. *See figure 10.* Let dry.

Step 9. With the #0 tip, pipe the embroidery. Stencil the top decoration and paint with gold. Attach the ribbon to the board.

Embellishments

Mini tiger lilies
Leaves
Dried babies' breath
Embroidery (See pattern illustration)

Embroidery pattern

$\mathscr{O}$ther Techniques and Designs

Here are a few different ways to decorate as well as some short cuts for those who want a cake in a hurry, including stencils, music boxes, masks and other unusual things.

Sporting Days Cake

Single Tier Hexagon

Step 1. Cover the board with fondant following instructions on page 91. Let dry overnight. Cover the cake with fondant and place on the board. With a #42 tip, pipe a small bead border around the base of the cake and let dry at least 4-5 days to harden the fondant.

Step 2. Make up black royal icing and, with a palette knife, spread the icing over the stencil. *See figure 1.* (Application of the stencil is made easier by tipping the cake slightly backwards. *See figure 2.*) When all six sides are stencilled, place the stencils on top of the cake and repeat. *See figure 3.*

figure 1

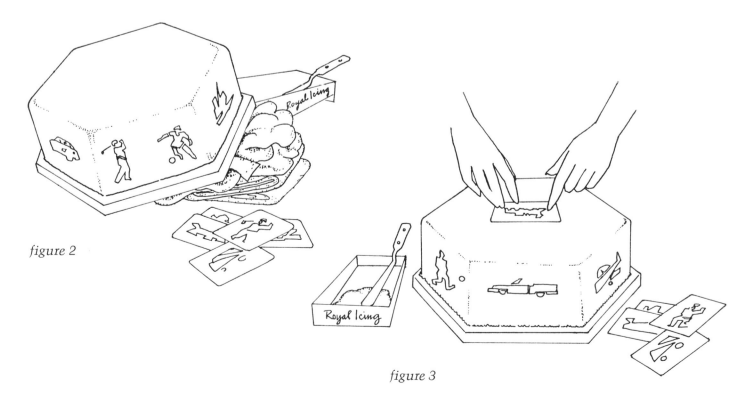

figure 2

figure 3

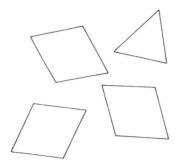

figure 1

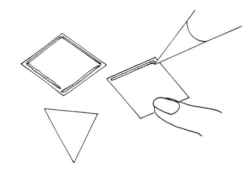

Harlequin Cake
Single Tier Hexagon

Step 1. Mix a small amount of white fondant into black fondant to get a marble effect and cover the cake board following instructions on page 91. Let dry overnight.

Step 2. With black fondant, roll out and cut a series of diamond shapes. *See figure 1.* Remove the black diamonds and, with royal icing, attach, from the top down, a line of diamonds. *See figure 2.* Roll out white fondant and repeat as above, this time attaching the white diamonds. *See figure 3.* Repeat, reversing the colours, until the cake is completed.

Step 3. With a #42 small open star tip, pipe a small border around the base of the cake. *See figure 4.*

Step 4. With red fondant, cover the top dome and attach to the cake. Pipe a small bead border around the base of the dome. *See figure 5.*

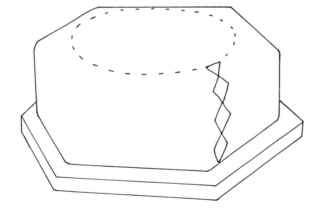

figure 2

white fondant

figure 3

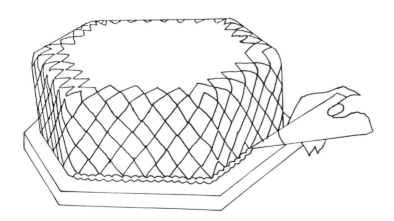

figure 4

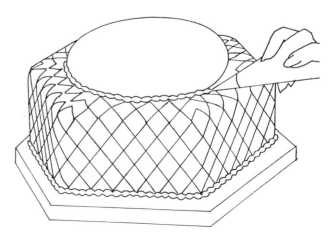

figure 5

Step 5. To make the masks, dust the inside of a porcelain mask with cornstarch. Roll out pastillage very thin and place inside the mask. *See figure 6.* Trim and cut out the eyes. Let dry overnight. Remove dry pastillage from mask and very gently sand the edges with an emery board or fine sandpaper. With a fine brush, paint the faces on the masks using a mixture of white alcohol and food colours. *See figure 7.* Set aside to dry. Attach 2 small pieces of ¹/₁₆″ coloured ribbon with royal icing to both inner sides of the masks at approximately ear level.

Step 6. Attach the masks to the cake, gently propping up the masks with cotton wool while the royal icing dries. *See figure 8.*

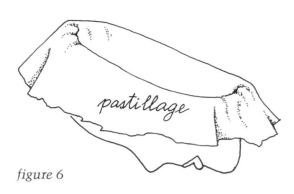

figure 6

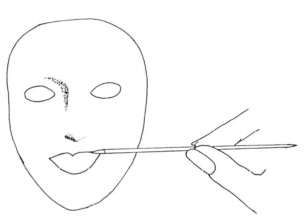

figure 7

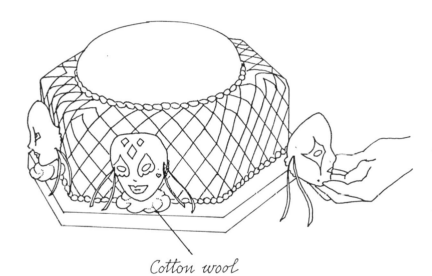

Cotton wool

figure 8

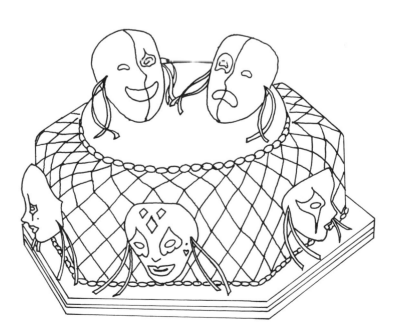

Black Classic Cake

3-Tier Square

A simple, elegant design that even beginners can master.

Step 1. Cover the board with fondant following instructions on page 91 and let dry overnight. Cover the cake with fondant and place on the board. With a #2 tip, pipe a small bead border around the base of the cake. While the fondant is very soft, using the top and bead border as your guide, crimp around the top and base of the cake. *See figure 1.* (As you crimp, occasionally wipe the ends of the crimper with white fat. This will prevent the crimper from sticking to the fondant. *See figure 2.* To make crimping easier, place either elastic bands or a nut and bolt through the crimper which will help it return to the same opening position.) Let dry overnight.

Step 2. With a #1 tip, pipe a straight line around the centre of the cake and, at the same time, apply the silver band.

Step 3. Apply 2 rows of thin ribbon on either side of the silver band. *See figure 3.* Repeat for the other 2 tiers.

Embellishments

Two lower tiers: silk anemones and pearls
Top tier: white metal stand-up stencils

figure 1

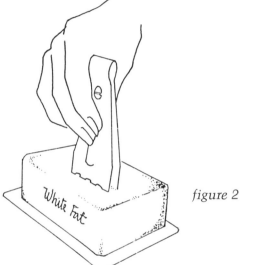

figure 2

White Fat

figure 3

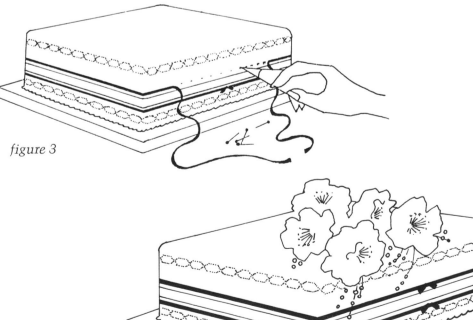

Sugar Music Box

Swans, shells, cards, boxes and toy boxes—any decorative item can be turned into a music box. Let your imagination be your guide.

Materials

Miniature music box mechanism and stand (easily obtainable from hobby or ceramic supply stores)
Pastillage ¹/₂ cup (see recipe, page 90)
Royal icing (small amount to glue box together)
Icing tip
Parchment bag
Florist oasis

Method

Step 1. Roll out a small amount of pastillage and place a thin layer on the base of the music box insert to provide an even level for working. Set aside.

Step 2. Colour the pastillage, then roll small pieces one at a time on cornstarch and cut out pieces. *See figure 1.* Place pieces on a flat surface to dry. Turn pieces frequently to prevent buckling. (Remember to cut a small hole in the centre of the base for insertion of music box.)

Step 3. When dry, sand edges with fine sandpaper. With a #1 tip, attach pieces together, using royal icing. Pipe inside the box to give added strength and let dry. Place a layer of royal icing on base of music box and place the musical movement in the bottom of the box. Pipe with a #1 tip around insert to reinforce, and allow to dry overnight.

Step 4. Fill empty box with florist oasis and arrange either gum paste or silk flowers in the foam.

Step 5. Attach lid using #1 tip and royal icing and keep lid propped open until dry.

Embellishments

Gum paste or silk flowers such as roses, blossoms, hyacinths

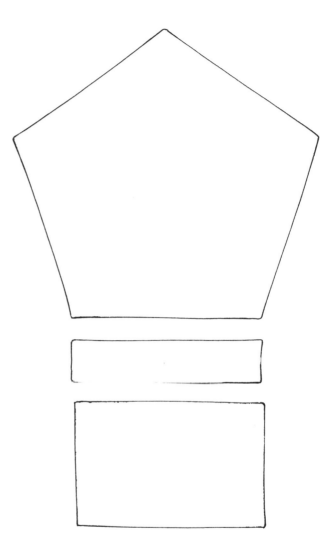

figure 1

Chapter 5

Wedding Cakes

What is more beautiful or elegant than a skilfully decorated wedding cake reflecting both traditional and modern influences.

White Classic Wedding Cake

3-Tier Hexagon

Step 1. Cover the board with fondant following instructions on page 91 and let dry overnight. Cover the cake with fondant and place on the board. With a #2 tip, pipe a small bead border around the base of the cake and let dry at least 1 hour.

Step 2. Make a false collar and place it around the cake making sure the collar is resting on the bead border. Very lightly, mark the pattern on the sides of the cake. *See figure 1.* Place two rows of white ribbon just above the marked line, attaching the ribbon with royal icing.

Step 3. With a #2 tip, pipe the scallop bridging for 6 lines. The first line must extend all the way around, while the 2nd, 3rd, 4th and 5th lines graduate ¹/₈" (3 mm) from both ends. Allow each line to dry before attempting the next line. The 6th line, like the first, must extend all the way around the cake. Let dry at least 3-4 hours, preferably overnight. *See figure 2.* With colour flow to the count of 10, colour flow the bridging. This both strengthens and hides the bridge work. Let dry 4 hours.

Step 4. With a #0 tip, pipe the strings from the middle marked line on the cake to the bridge. *See figure 3.* Let dry while making lace pieces.

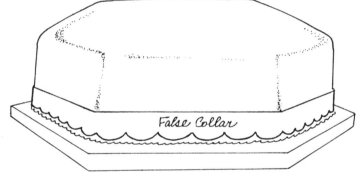

figure 1

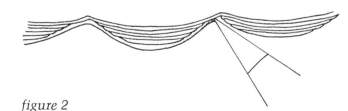

figure 2

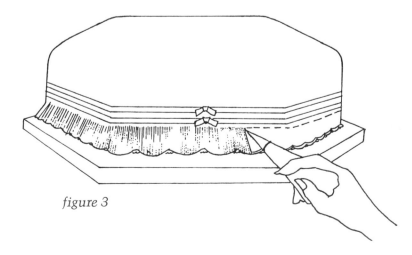

figure 3

Step 5. With royal icing blended to a thinner consistency, pipe rain drops on the string work, taking care not to break the strings. *See figure 4.* Pipe 2 dots on one string, then miss a string, then pipe 3 dots on the next string. Repeat the pattern all around the cake.

Step 6. Attach the lace pieces either by applying small dots or a small bead border to the top of the strings using a #0 tip. (Do not pipe a very large section at a time or the dots will dry.) *See figure 5.*

Step 7. With a #0 tip, pipe the embroidery and let dry. With a #0 tip, pipe small scallops around the base of the strings and let dry. With a small pin, attach white ribbon around the base of the cake boards. Repeat for the other 2 tiers.

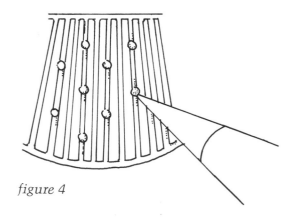

figure 4

Embellishments

Note: For instructions on how to arrange the flowers for this cake, see the chapter on step-by-step flower arrangements.

Ivy leaves

White roses

White stephanotis

White cymbidium orchids with peach throat and pearls

Embroidery (See pattern illustration)

figure 5

Embroidery pattern

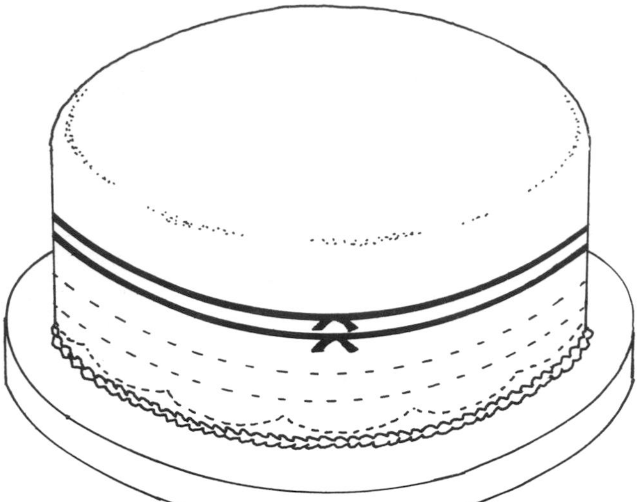

figure 1

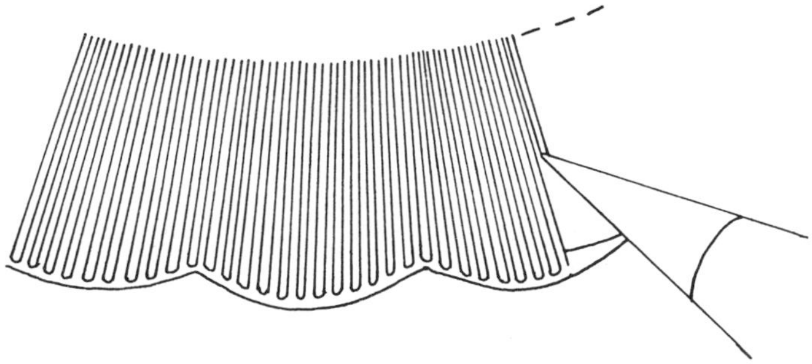

Masquerade Wedding Cake
3-Tier Round

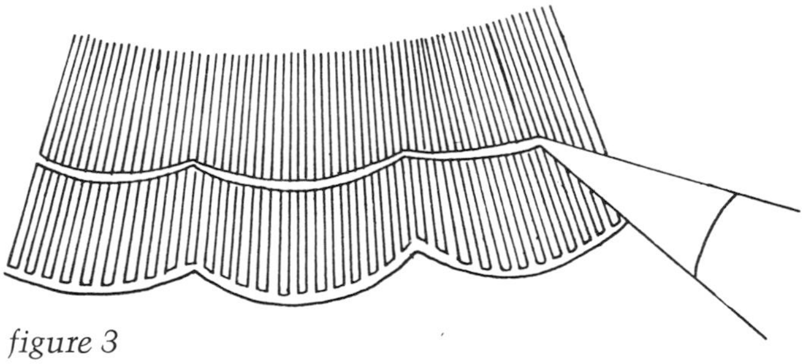

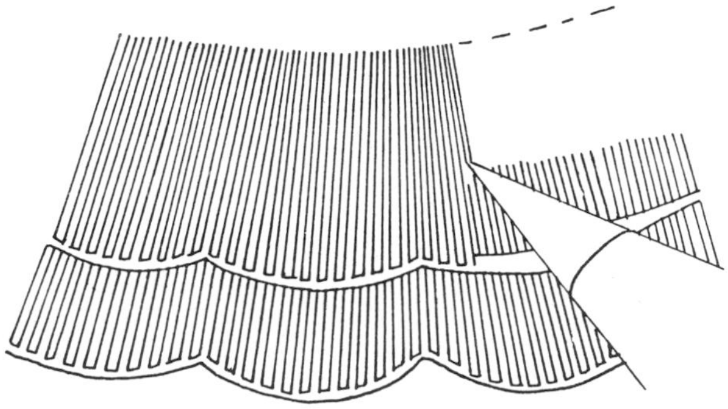

A cake designed for a Hallowe'en wedding featuring pastillage masks.

Step 1. Cover the boards with fondant following instructions on page 91 and let dry overnight. Cover the cakes with fondant and place the cakes on the boards. With a #2 tip, pipe a small bead border around the base of the cakes and let dry. Attach 2 rows of black ribbon to each tier.

Step 2. Make a false collar to fit the cakes and mark two solid lines around the middle of the cake. *See figure 1.* Pipe the bridging with a #2 tip. Let dry . Flood in the bridging with black royal icing and let dry at least 4 hours.

Step 3. With a #0 tip, pipe strings from the lowest line attaching the strings to the bridging. Continue all the way around the cake and let dry 4 hours. *See figure 2.* Once dry, with a #2 tip and white royal icing, pipe a scallop approximately half way up the strings, *See figure 3,* and when you have piped one scallop all the way around the cake, pipe 4 more scallops on top of the first scallop. Let dry overnight. Flood in with white royal icing. (Extra care must be taken when flooding as the back strings cannot be repaired if they are broken.) Let dry. With a #0 tip, pipe strings from the top marked line to the new bridging. Let dry. *See figure 4.*

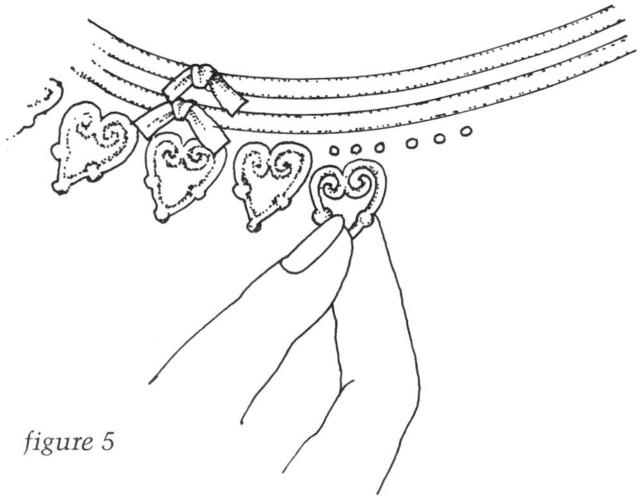

figure 2

figure 4

figure 5

figure 3

Step 4. With a #0 tip, pipe the lace pieces onto cooking film or plastic, this time piping extra pieces to allow for the top row of lace pieces.

Let dry. When dry, attach lace pieces by applying small dots of icing to the cake and attaching the lace pieces. *See figure 5.* Also, attach the lace pieces to the top edge of the cake. With a #0 tip, pipe the rows of scallops to both edges of the strings. *See figure 6.* Repeat for the other two tiers. Attach the ribbon around the sides of the boards.

Embellishments

Light cream roses
White moth orchids
White epidendrum
Ivy leaves
Pearls

Embroidery: small dots around the top lace pieces

To Make Pastillage Masks

Follow instructions in Step 5 of Harlequin Cake on page 33.

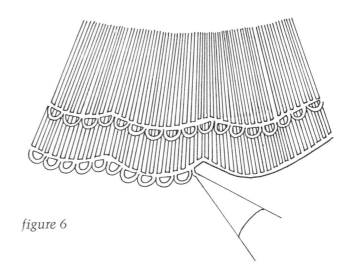

figure 6

figure 1

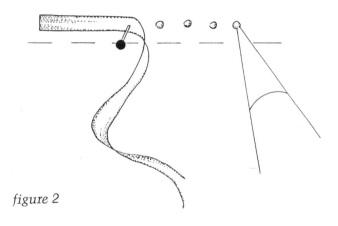

figure 2

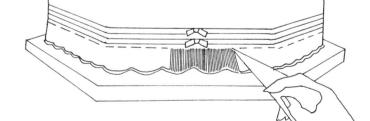

figure 3

Ivory Wedding Cake

2-Tier Hexagon

Step 1. Cover the board with fondant following instructions on page 91 and let dry overnight. Cover the cake with fondant and place on the board. With a #2 tip, pipe a small bead border around the base of the cake and let dry at least 1 hour.

Step 2. Make a false collar and place it around the cake making sure the collar is resting on the bead border. Very lightly, mark the pattern on the side of the cake. *See figure 1.* Place two rows of white ribbon just above the marked line, attaching the ribbon with royal icing. *See figure 2.*

Step 3. With a #2 tip, pipe the scallop bridging for 6 lines. The first line must extend all the way around, while the 2nd, 3rd, 4th and 5th lines graduate ¹/₈″ (3 mm) from both ends. Allow each line to dry before attempting the next line. The 6th line, like the first, must extend all the way around the cake. Let dry at least 3-4 hours, preferably overnight. With colour flow to the count of 10, colour flow the bridging. This both strengthens and hides the bridge work. Let dry 4 hours.

Step 4. With a #0 tip, pipe the strings from the middle marked line on the cake to the bridge. *See figure 3.* Let dry while making lace pieces.

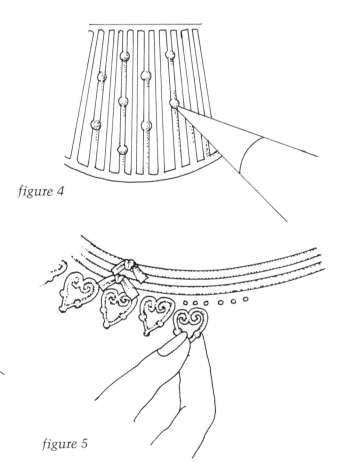

figure 4

figure 5

WHITE CLASSIC WEDDING CAKE

MASQUERADE WEDDING CAKE

IVORY WEDDING CAKE

CANDLELIGHT WEDDING CAKE

Step 5. With royal icing blended to a thinner consistency, pipe rain drops on the string work, taking care not to break the strings. *See figure 4*. Pipe 2 dots on one string then miss a string, then 3 dots on the next string. Repeat the pattern all around the cake.

Step 6. Attach the lace pieces either by applying small dots or a small bead border to the top of the strings using a #0 tip. (Do not pipe a very large section at a time or the dots will dry.) *See figure 5*.

Step 7. With a #0 tip, pipe the embroidery and let dry. With a #0 tip, pipe small scallops around the base of the strings and let dry. With a small pin, attach white ribbon around the base of the cake boards. Repeat for the other tier.

Embellishments

White stephanotis
White sweet peas
White freesia
Cymbidium orchids
Silk leaves
Pearl leaves
Sprays of pearls
Embroidery (See pattern illustration)

Embroidery pattern

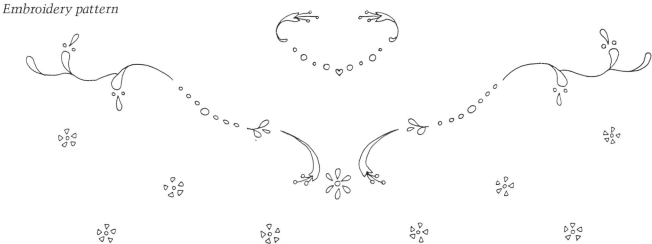

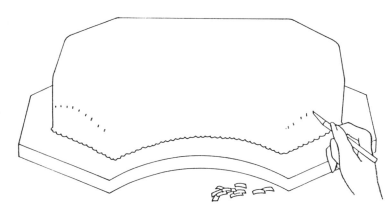

figure 1

figure 2

Candlelight Wedding Cake

3-Tier Long Octagonal with semi-circular cut out

I designed this cake for an article in *Canadian Bride Magazine*. It was made in an 8-sided oblong tin set with a half circle of wood placed in the tins before baking. *See figure 1.*

Step 1. Cover the boards with fondant following instructions on page 91 and let dry overnight. Cover the cakes with fondant and place on the boards. With a #2 tip, pipe a small bead border around the bases of the cakes. Let dry.

Step 2. Make a false collar, place on cake and mark the pattern onto the cake. See instructions on page 92. Remove collar. Using an x-acto knife, cut small slits through the fondant just above the marked pattern, approximately 1/2″ (13 mm) apart, all around the 7 sides of the cake to allow for placement of the ribbon. *See figure 2.*

Step 3. With a #2 tip, pipe the scallop bridging for 6 lines. The first line must extend all the way around the cake while the 2nd, 3rd, 4th and 5th lines graduate 1/8″ (3 mm) from both ends. Allow each line to dry before attempting the next line. The 6th line, like the first, must extend all the way around the cake. Let dry. With colour flow to the count of 10, colour flow the bridging. This both strengthens and hides the bridgework. Let dry at least 4 hours. *See figure 3.*

figure 3

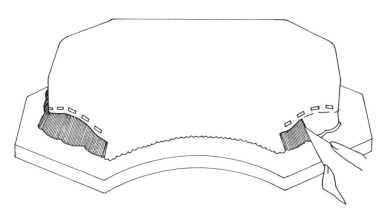

figure 4

Step 4. With a #0 tip, pipe the strings down from the pattern to the bridge. Let dry. *See figure 4.* To pipe the central crossover design of each scallop, count 5 strings of icing in the centre of the pattern and, with a #0 tip, pipe a zigzag line from the first string to the centre string of each scalloped pattern. *See figure 5.* Then pipe from the 5th string back to the centre to form a diamond. *See figure 6.* Let dry.

Step 5. With a #0 tip, pipe very small dots on the centre and each point of the diamond pattern. With a #0 tip, pipe the lace pieces onto a small sheet of thin plastic or cooking film. Let dry. To attach the lace pieces to the cake, pipe either a small bead border or very small dots onto the top of the strings and, very gently, attach the lace pieces to the dots.

Step 6. With a #0 tip, pipe the embroidery pattern. Let dry.

Step 7. With a small pin, attach white ribbon around the base of the cake boards and arrange the flowers on top of the cakes. Repeat for the other tier. Place the candles on the lower tier.

figure 5

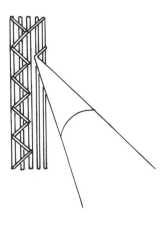

figure 6

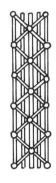

Embellishments

Peach rose
White cattleya orchids
Silk leaves
Pearls
Embroidery (See pattern illustration)
Lace pieces

Embroidery pattern

Cushion Heart Wedding Cake

3-Tier Heart Shape

A soft, delicate cake embellished with fresh flowers.

Step 1. Cover boards with fondant following instructions on page 91 and let dry overnight. Cover the 2 side cakes with fondant and place on the boards. Cover the lower half of the bottom tier with fondant and trim around the cake. *See figure 1.* Then cover the top half of the cake with fondant, joining the seams together with a smoother. *See figure 2.* Place cake on the board, and with a #2 tip, pipe a small bead border around the bases of the cakes.

Step 2. For the lower tier, make a template to fit inside the top of the cake. Leaving the template on top of the cake, proceed with the ribbon insertion. *See figure 3.* (See step 4 on page 64.)

Step 3. With a #0 tip, pipe at an angle a line ¹/₂″ long all around the sides of the cake. *See figure 4.* When completed, pipe another line of equal length in the opposite direction to make a crisscross design. *See figure 5.* Continue overpiping, making each line of piping approximately ¹/₄″ longer at each end. *See figure 6.*

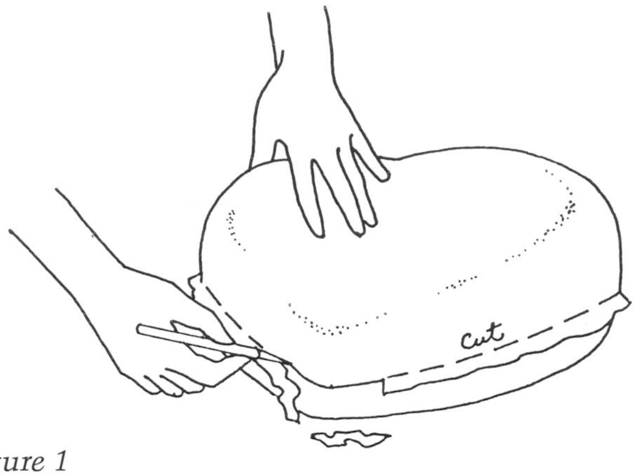

figure 1

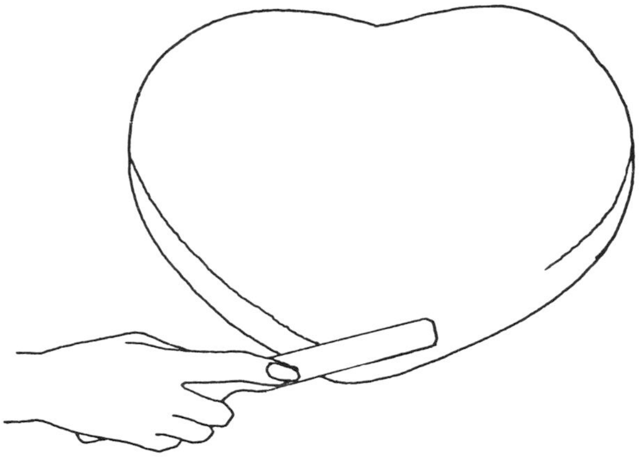

figure 2

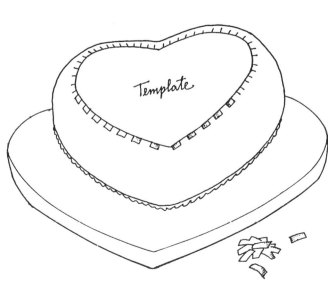

figure 3

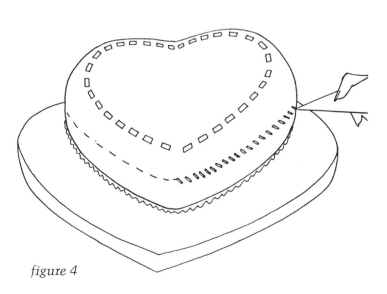

figure 4

Step 4. Continue with the overpiping for at least 6-8 complete patterns. (One pattern equals one complete row of crisscrosses.) Roll out fondant and cut a narrow frill. Place on a cornstarch board and ruffle along one edge. (See step 2 on page 63.) With a #1 tip, pipe a small bead border around the base of the overpiping, and attach the frill. *See figure 7.* To cover the join seam, pipe a small bead border on top of the frill join. *See figure 8.*

Step 5. With a #0 tip, pipe lace pieces and let dry. With a #0 tip, pipe a small bead border around the top of the overpiping and, at the same time, attach the lace pieces. Place ribbon around the board.

Step 6. With a frill cutter, cut out frills and place on a cornstarch board. With an anger tool or round toothpick, ruffle the frill. *See figure 9.*

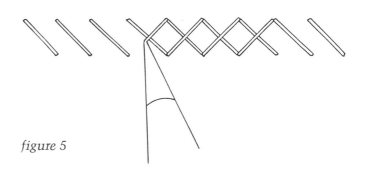

figure 5

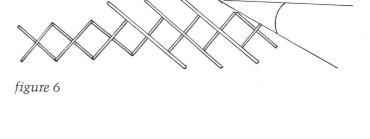

figure 6

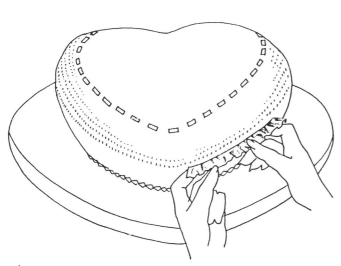

figure 7

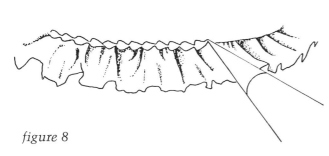

figure 8

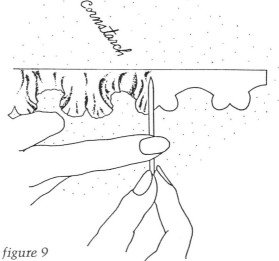

figure 9

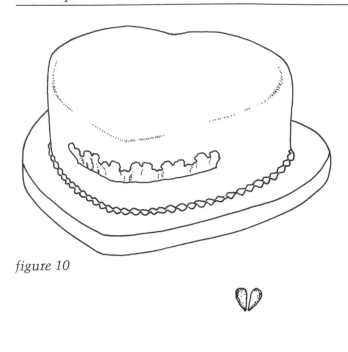

figure 10

Step 7. Pipe a line of royal icing along the top edge of the frill and, with the frill turned upside down, place just below the middle of the cake. *See figure 10.* Continue with 2 more rows. To finish the cake, place 2 rows of ribbon around the base of the cakes.

Step 8. With a #1 tip, pipe two beads to form a heart around the top of the cake. *See figure 11.* Pipe small birds on cooking film. *See figure 12.* When dry, attach to the cake.

Step 9. To dust the edges of the frills, place wax paper on top of the board and, with a #9 or #10 paint brush, gently dust the tips of the ruffles, taking care not to get dust on the boards. Place ribbon around boards.

Embellishments

Fresh white tiger lilies
Nerine lilies
White carnations and greenery (Place in vases and then on cakes.)
Embroidery birds and hearts (See figures 11 and 12)
Frill (See pattern illustration)

figure 11

figure 12

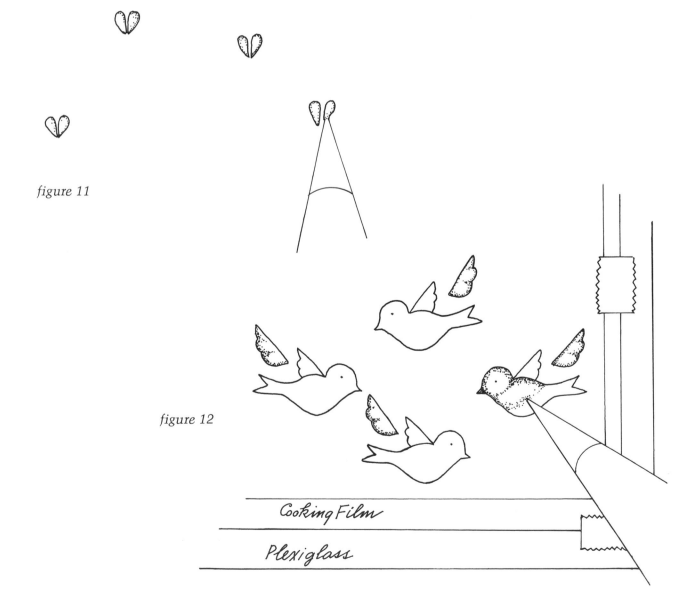

Cooking Film

Plexiglass

Frill pattern

legance

Graceful lines, a presentation that combines style and flair and perfect colours ensure that "elegance is in the eye of the beholder."

Love Bird Cake

Single Tier Scalloped Oval

Two graceful love birds—a stunning new design any bride and groom will cherish.

Step 1. Cover the board with fondant following instructions on page 91 and let dry overnight. Cover the cake with fondant and place on the board. With a #2 tip, pipe a small bead border around the base of the cake and let dry at least 1 hour.

Step 2. Make a false collar and place it around the cake making sure the collar is resting on the bead border. Very lightly, mark the pattern on the side of the cake. *See figure 1.*

Step 3. With a #2 tip, pipe the scallop bridging for 6 lines. (See figures 10 and 11 on pages 93 and 94.) Let dry. Flood the bridge in and dry at least 3-4 hours or overnight.

Step 4. With a #0 tip, pipe the strings from the middle marked line on the cake to the bridge. *See figure 2.* Let dry while making lace pieces.

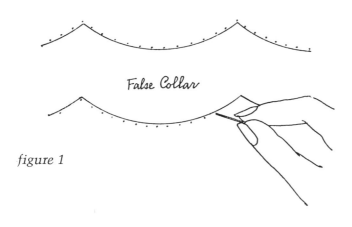

False Collar

figure 1

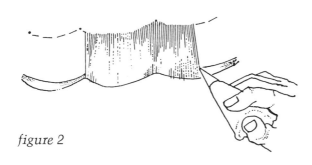

figure 2

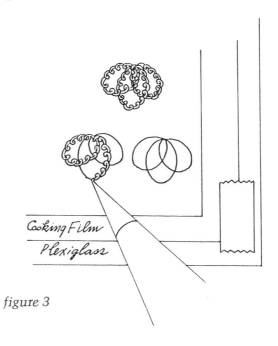

Cooking Film
Plexiglass

figure 3

CUSHION HEART WEDDING CAKE

LOVE BIRD CAKE

FANTASY CAKE

BLACK ENCHANTMENT CAKE

Step 5. With a #0 tip, pipe the embroidery onto cooking film. *See figure 3.*

Step 6. With a #0 tip, attach the lace pieces. Let dry.

Step 7. Pipe a small scallop around the base of the strings. *See figure 4.* Attach ribbon to base of the board.

Step 8. Place birds on top of the cake.

To Make the Birds

Step 1. Wipe the molds clean with a dry cloth and place on a sheet of wax silicone paper. Bring to the boil: 625 g. sugar; 250 g. water; 100 g. glucose. Boil to 120°C; add 1/2 tsp. white white then boil to 152°C. Place the saucepan into a larger saucepan of cold water to stop the sugar from cooking. Then add food colour to the sugar mixture with a toothpick. Rotate the saucepan until the colour marbles. Remove saucepan from cold water. Then, very carefully, pour into the molds, covering the bottom no more than 1/4'' deep. *See figure 5.* Let cool.

Step 2. To release the birds, gently pull the molds away from the sugar birds and stands. *See figure 6.*

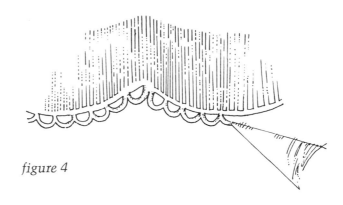

figure 4

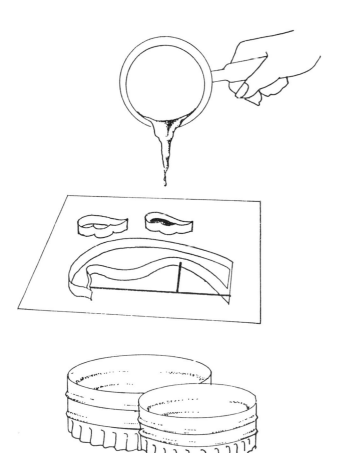

figure 5

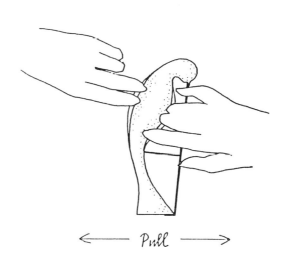

← Pull →

figure 6

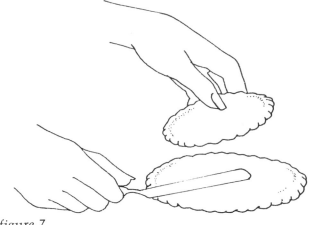

figure 7

Step 3. With a knife heated over the flame of a butane torch, assemble the base, *See figure 7*, then the birds. Attach the back wing first, then the front wing. *See figure 8.* (Each time, reheat the knife, wiping on a damp cloth.) Then, attach the birds to the base. *See figure 9.*

Embellishments

Embroidery (See pattern illustration)
Lace pieces (Patterns from *Brazilian Three-Dimensional Embroidery* by Rosie Montague.)

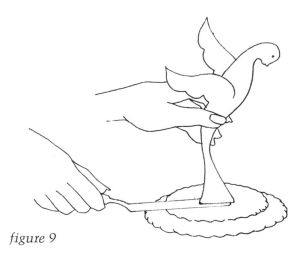

figure 9

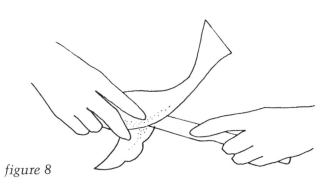

figure 8

Embroidery pattern

Fantasy Cake

Single Tier Oval

The Rolls-Royce of cake decorating and the most difficult and challenging cake I have ever decorated, not only because black icing is used, but because the design carries over onto the top edge of the cake.

Step 1. Cover the board with fondant following instructions on page 91 and let dry overnight. Cover the cake with fondant following instructions on page 92 and place on the board. Pipe a small bead border around the base of the cake. Let dry at least 1 hour.

Step 2. With a false collar, mark the pattern onto the sides of the cake using a pin or dressmaker's wheel. Remove the collar and with a #2 tip, pipe the bridging on the lower pattern only. *See figure 1.* Let dry. Flood in the bridge with black icing taking care not to overfill the bridge. Let dry. With a #0 tip, pipe the strings from the lower pattern mark to the bridge. Let dry. *See figure 2.* Then pipe the 3 lines of scallops.

Step 3. With a #2 tip, repeat, piping the next bridging, allowing it to dry before flooding in the bridge. Let dry. With a #0 tip, pipe the strings from the next marked pattern line to the bridge. Let dry.

Step 4. Repeat again, piping the bridge. Let dry. Flood in and let dry. Pipe the 3rd pattern of strings. Let dry. Again, pipe the 3 rows of scallops. Let dry.

Step 5. Repeat again, piping the final bridge at the top of the cake. Let dry. Flood in and let dry. With a cloth under the board to raise the cake, pipe the strings from the marked pattern line to the bridge. *See figure 3.* (This line of strings is very difficult to pipe as the strings want to fall down onto the top edge of the cake.) Let dry.

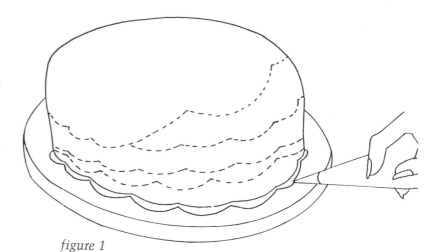

figure 1

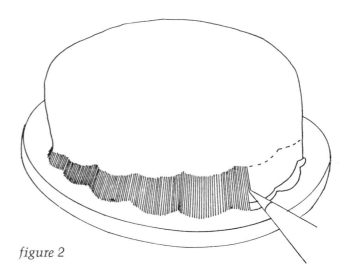

figure 2

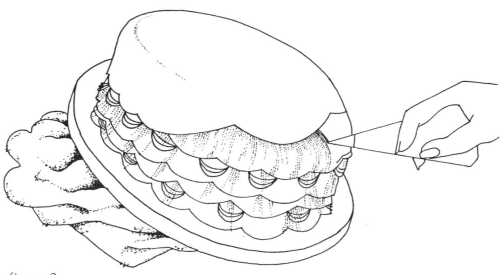

figure 3

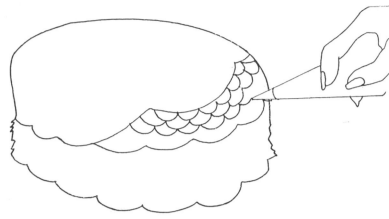

figure 4

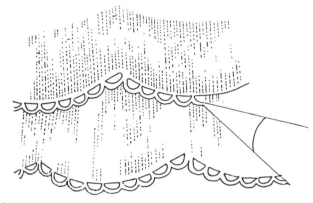

figure 5

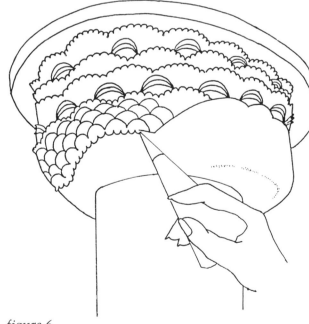

figure 6

Step 6. With a #0 tip, pipe the small scallops on top of the final strings. Remove the cloth from under the board. *See figure 4.*

Step 7. With a #0 tip, pipe the small scallop around all the bridging. *See figure 5.* When dry, very carefully turn the cake upside down and stand the cake on a large tin or glass jar. Continue piping the small scallops all around the top edge of the cake. *See figure 6.* Let dry. Very gently turn the cake right side up.

Step 8. With a #0 tip, pipe the embroidery around both sides of the cake. Let dry. To finish the cake, attach ribbon to the sides of the board. Place feathers, flowers on top of the cake.

Embellishments

White cattleya orchids
Silk black filler flowers
Silk and pearl leaves
White feathers
Embroidery (See pattern illustration)

Embroidery pattern

Black Enchantment Cake

Single Tier Round

A world traveller, this cake went to England for the London Show in December 1986, to Indianapolis in August 1987 and finally to Japan in February 1988.

Step 1. Cover the board with fondant following instructions on page 91 and let dry overnight. Cover the cake with fondant, placing the cake on the board. With a #2 tip, pipe a small bead border around the base of the cake and let dry. Attach 2 rows of black ribbon to the cake.

Step 2. Make a false collar to fit the cake and mark two solid lines around the middle of the cake. *See figure 1.* Pipe the bridging with a #2 tip. Let dry . Flood in the bridging with black royal icing and let dry at least 4 hours.

Step 3. With a #0 tip, pipe strings from the lowest line attaching the strings to the bridging. Continue all the way around the cake and let dry 4 hours. *See figure 2.* Once dry, with a #2 tip and white royal icing, pipe a scallop approximately half way up the strings, *See figure 3,* and when you have piped one scallop all the way around the cake, pipe 4 more scallops on top of the first scallop. Let dry overnight. Flood in with white royal icing. (Extra care must be taken when flooding as the back strings cannot be repaired if they are broken.) Let dry. With a #0 tip, pipe strings from the top marked line to the new bridging. Let dry. *See figure 4.*

figure 1

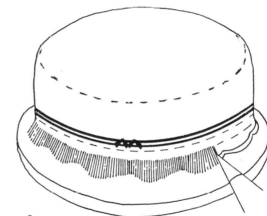

figure 2

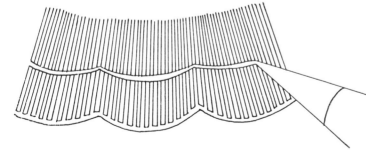

figure 3

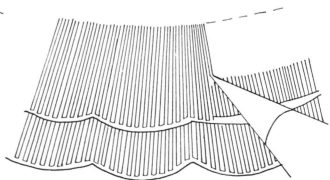

figure 4

Step 4. With a #0 tip and white royal icing, pipe the lace pieces onto cooking film or plastic. Repeat step, this time overpiping in black royal icing. Pipe extra pieces to allow for the top row of lace pieces. *See figure 5.* Let dry. When dry, attach lace pieces by applying small dots of icing to the cake and attaching the lace pieces. *See figure 6.* Also, attach the lace pieces to the top edge of the cake. Attach the ribbon around the side of the board.

Embellishments

Moth orchids attached to ribbon pull bows
Embroidery: small dots around the top lace pieces
Lace pieces (See figure 5)

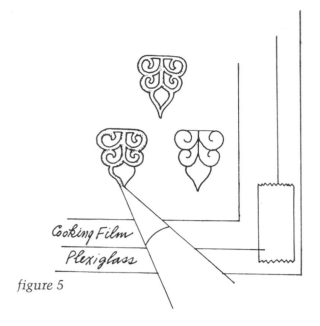

Cooking Film
Plexiglass

figure 5

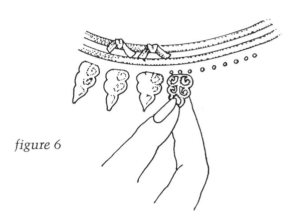

figure 6

Chapter 7

*R*uffles

Brides love the feminine look of ruffles on a truly traditional wedding cake. There are so many ways to decorate with ruffles and they are fast and practical for beginners and commercial pastry chefs.

White Beauty Ruffle Cake

3-Tier Hexagon

Step 1. Cover the boards with fondant following instructions on page 91 and let dry overnight. Cover the cakes with fondant and place on the boards. With a #2 tip, pipe a small bead border around the base of the cakes. Let dry overnight.

Step 2. Cut sections of fondant (to which gum tragacanth has been added unless a commercial fondant is being used) with a frill cutter. Cut off the scalloped edge to form a straight edge frill. *See figure 1.* Place the frill on a dusted cornstarch board and, with an anger tool, round toothpick or cocktail stick, ruffle one edge. *See figure 2.* Dust off excess cornstarch. With a #2 tip, pipe royal icing along the centre of the ruffle. *See figure 3.* Attach to the cake and continue applying the sections until the lower ruffle is completed. You may wish to put small pieces of tissue paper under the ruffle to hold their shape until semi-dry. *See figure 4.*

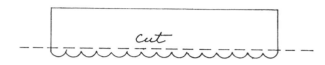

figure 1

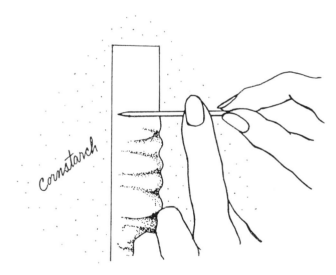

figure 2

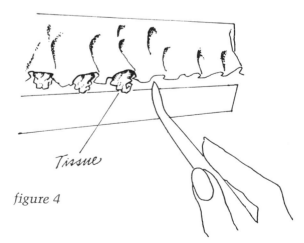

Tissue

figure 4

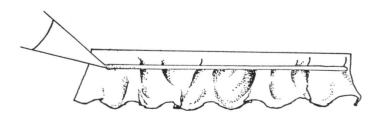

figure 3

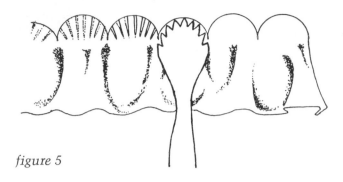

figure 5

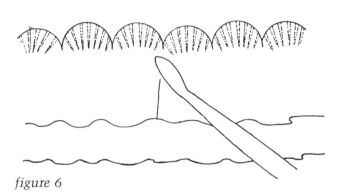

figure 6

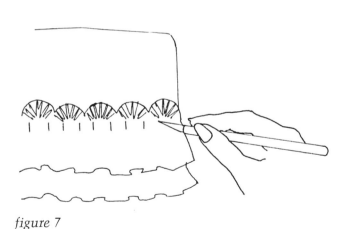

figure 7

Step 3. Cut out the top ruffle, leaving the scallop attached. Ruffle the lower edge and, with a fan tool, press the design into each scallop. *See figure 5*. Apply the top ruffle with royal icing. This time when seaming the pieces together, pipe a small section of icing down the centre of both seams and smoothen with a palette knife or smooth-edged tool. *See figure 6*.

Step 4. Using an x-acto knife, cut small slits through the fondant approximately ¹/₂″ (13 mm) apart all around the cake to allow for insertion of the ribbon. Cut small sections of ribbon (to be inserted into the slits on the cake) slightly longer than the width between the slits to allow the ribbon ends to tuck easily into the slits. *See figure 7*.

Step 5. Mark embroidery and pipe with a #0 tip. Repeat for other 2 tiers.

Embellishments

Stephanotis
Moth orchids
Pearls
Silk leaves
Embroidery (See pattern illustration)

Embroidery pattern

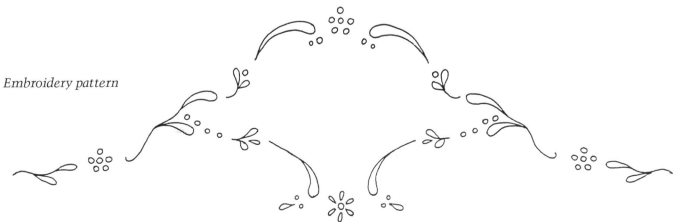

WHITE BEAUTY RUFFLE CAKE

LILAC RUFFLE CAKE

JEWEL RUFFLE CAKE

VICTORIAN POSY RUFFLE CAKE

Lilac Ruffle Cake

3-Tier Hexagon

A beautiful cake featuring ruffles and an icing bride and groom.

Step 1. Cover the boards with fondant following instructions on page 91 and let dry overnight. Cover the cakes with fondant and place on the boards. With a #2 tip, pipe a small bead border around the base of the cakes. Let dry overnight.

Step 2. Cut sections of fondant (to which gum tragacanth has been added unless a commercial fondant is being used) with a frill cutter. Cut off the scalloped edge to form a straight edge frill. *See figure 1.* Place the frill on a dusted cornstarch board and, with an anger tool, round toothpick or cocktail stick, ruffle one edge. *See figure 2.* Dust off excess cornstarch. With a #2 tip, pipe royal icing along the centre of the ruffle. *See figure 3.* Attach to the cake and continue applying the sections until the lower ruffle is completed. You may wish to put small pieces of tissue paper under the ruffle to hold their shape until semi-dry. *See figure 4.*

Step 3. Cut out the top ruffle, leaving the scallop attached. Ruffle the lower edge and, with a fan tool, press the design into each scallop. *See figure 5.*

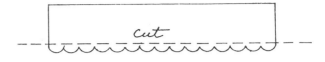

figure 1

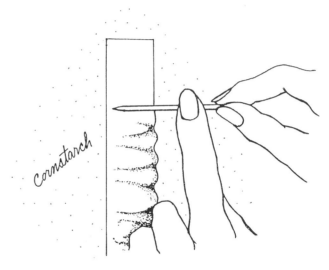

figure 2

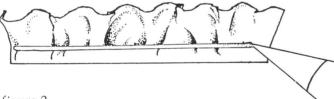

figure 3

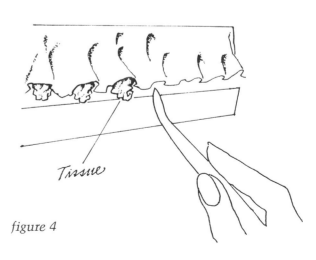

figure 4

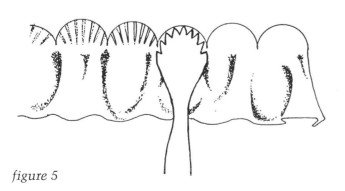

figure 5

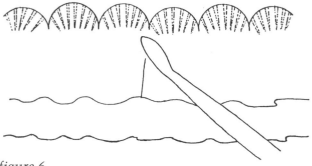

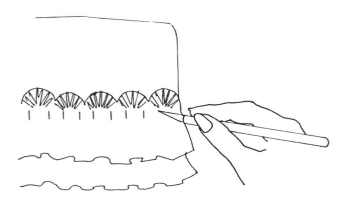

figure 6

figure 7

Apply the top ruffle with royal icing. This time when seaming the pieces together, pipe a small section of icing down the centre of both seams and smoothen with a palette knife or smooth-edged tool. *See figure 6.*

Step 4. Using an x-acto knife, cut small slits through the fondant approximately 1/2″ (13 mm) apart all around the cake to allow for insertion of the ribbon. Cut small sections of ribbon (to be inserted into the slits on the cake) slightly longer than the width between the slits to allow the ribbon ends to tuck easily into the slits. *See figure 7.*

Step 5. Mark embroidery and pipe with a #0 tip. Repeat for other 2 tiers.

For instructions on how to make the bride and groom, see page 80.

Embellishments

Roses
Stephanotis
Cattleya orchids
Babies' breath
Spray of mauve forget-me-nots
Silk pearl leaves
Pearls
Embroidery (See pattern illustration)

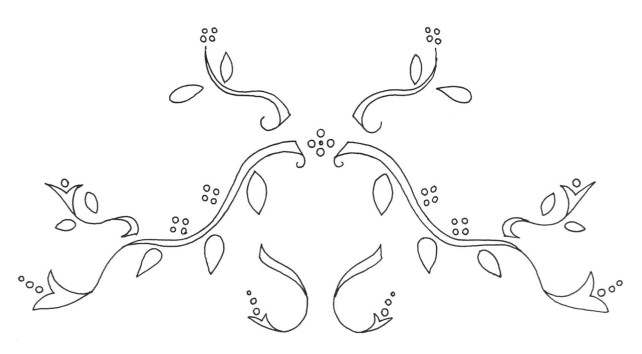

Embroidery pattern

Jewel Ruffle Cake

3-Tier Petal

The same ruffles can give each style of cake a totally different look. This cake is the same design as the White Beauty Ruffle Cake with the added touch of an antique jewel box.

Step 1. Cover the boards with fondant following instructions on page 91 and let dry overnight. Cover the cakes with fondant and place on the boards. With a #2 tip, pipe a small bead border around the base of the cakes. Let dry overnight.

Step 2. Cut sections of fondant (to which gum tragacanth has been added unless commercial fondant is being used) with a frill cutter. Cut off the scalloped edge to form a straight edge frill. *See figure 1.* Place the frill onto a dusted cornstarch board and, with an anger tool, round toothpick or cocktail stick, ruffle one edge. *See figure 2.* Dust off excess cornstarch. With a #2 tip, pipe royal icing along the centre of the ruffle. *See figure 3.* Attach to the cake and continue applying the sections until the lower ruffle is completed. You may wish to put small pieces of tissue paper under the ruffle to hold their shape until semi-dry. *See figure 4.*

Step 3. Cut out the top ruffle, leaving the scallop attached. Ruffle the lower edge and with a fan tool press the design into each scallop. *See figure 5.* Apply the top ruffle with royal icing. This time, when seaming the pieces together, pipe a small section of icing down the centre of both seams and smoothen with a palette knife or smooth-edged tool. *See figure 6.*

figure 1

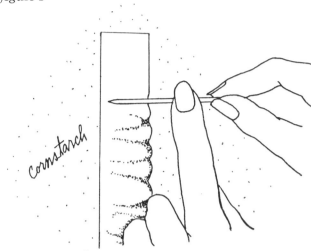

figure 2

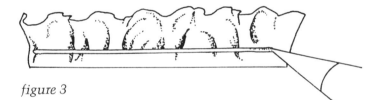

figure 3

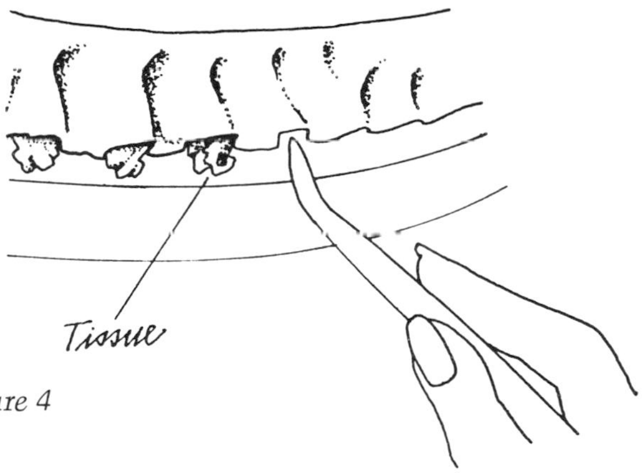

figure 4

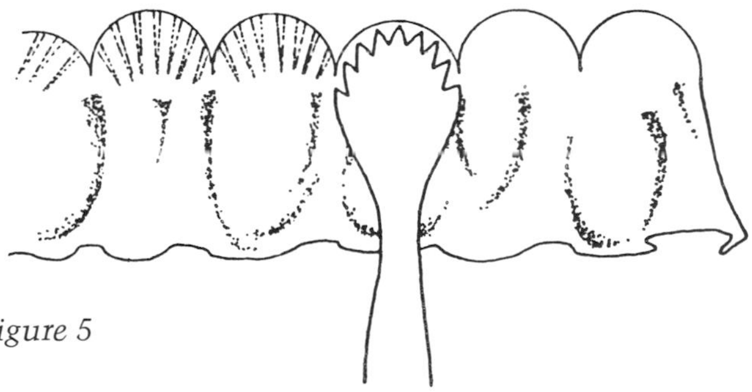

figure 5

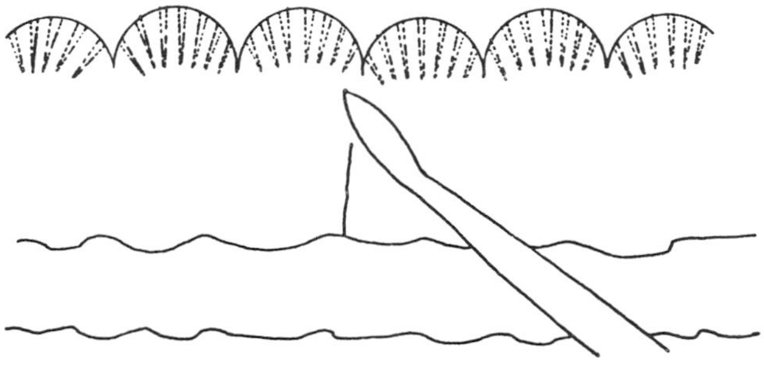

figure 6

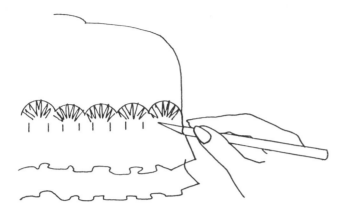

figure 7

Step 4. Using an x-acto knife, cut small slits through the fondant approximately ¹/₂″ (13 mm) apart all around the cake to allow for insertion of the ribbon. Cut small sections of ribbon (to be inserted into the slits on the cake) slightly longer than the width between the slits to allow the ribbon ends to tuck easily into the slits. See figure 7.

Step 5. Mark embroidery and pipe with a #0 tip. Repeat for other 2 tiers.

Embellishments

Peach roses
Stephanotis
Ivy leaves
White roses
Gardenias
Embroidery (See pattern illustration)

Embroidery pattern

Victorian Posy Ruffle Cake

3-Tier Scalloped Oval

Lots of ruffles, lace pieces, and Victorian posy flower holders compliment this unusual way with a double ruffle.

Step 1. Cover the board with fondant following instructions on page 91 and let dry overnight. Cover the cakes with fondant and place on the boards. Let dry overnight.

Step 2. With a straight frill cutter, roll out and cut a fondant ruffle. *See figure 1.* Place the frill on a dusted cornstarch board and, with an anger tool or a round toothpick, ruffle both edges. *See figure 2.* Cut the frill in half. *See figure 3.*

Step 3. With a #2 tip, pipe royal icing along the cut edge of the frill. *See figure 4.* Attach to the base of the cake. Continue applying the sections until the lower ruffle is completed.

Step 4. Cut out the top ruffle and attach it to the cake remembering to leave approximately a ¹⁄₂″ (1.5 cm) space between the top and lower ruffle. Continue attaching the ruffle until the cake is completed. *See figure 5.* With a #2 tip, pipe a small bead border around the base of the cake. *See figure 6.* Let dry.

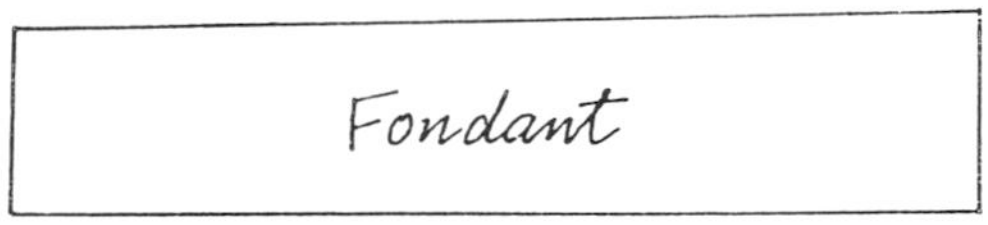

figure 1

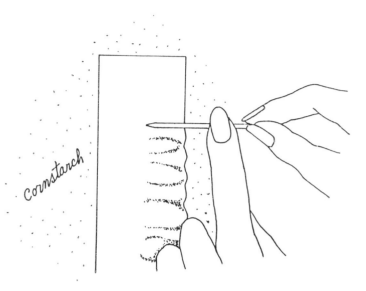

figure 2

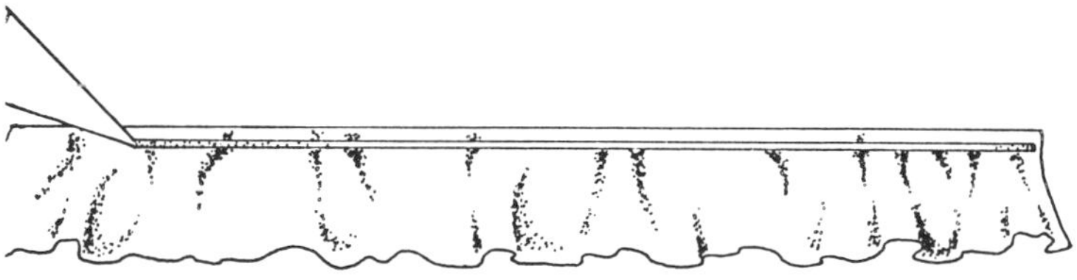

figure 4

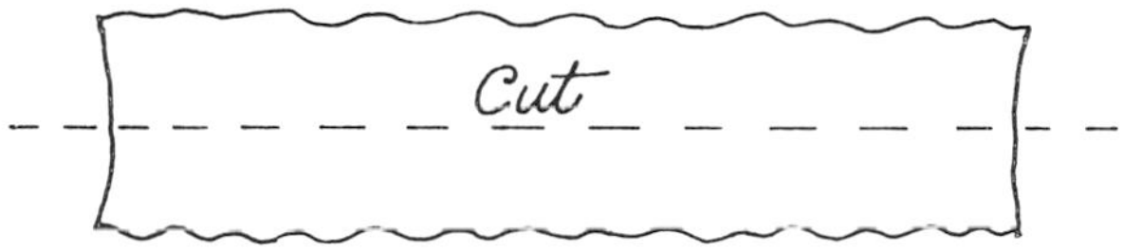

figure 3

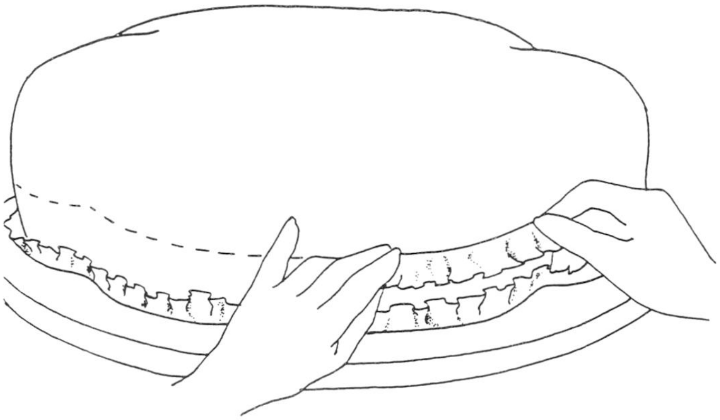

figure 5

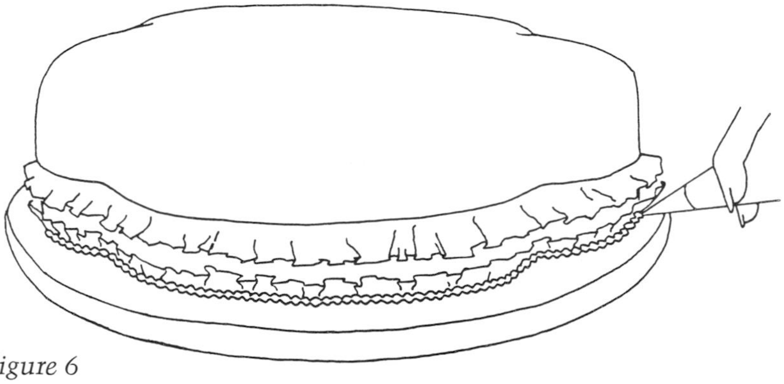

figure 6

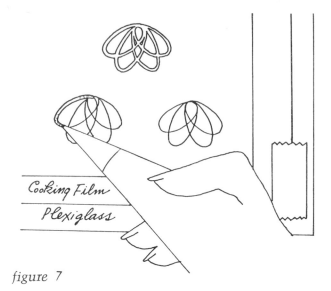

figure 7

Cooking Film

Plexiglass

Step 5. With a #0 tip, pipe the lace pieces, *See figure 7*, and let dry. Attach the two rows of ribbon. With a #0 tip, pipe a very small bead border around the top ruffle. Attach all the lace pieces, remembering to work with no more than 4 pieces at a time.

Step 6. With a #0 tip, pipe the embroidery patterns on the cakes. Let dry. Place the ribbons around the cake boards.

Embellishments

For instructions on how to arrange the flowers for this cake, see the chapter on step-by-step flower arrangements.
Rosebuds
Roses
Open blown roses
Silk leaves
Pearls
Lace and ribbon posy holders
Gum paste painted butterflies
Embroidery (See pattern illustration)
Lace pieces (*See figure 7*)

Embroidery pattern

Ivory and Pearls Ruffle Cake

3-Tier Oval

For ruffle lovers, a unique design featuring upside-down double ruffles with an icing bride and groom. The icing bride's dress has 3 layers of fine ruffles.

Step 1. Cover the board with fondant following instructions on page 91 and let dry overnight. Cover the cakes with fondant and place on the boards. Let dry overnight. Attach bride and groom to cake with royal icing (see instructions on how to make bride and groom on page 80).

Step 2. With a straight frill cutter, roll out and cut a fondant ruffle. *See figure 1.* Place the frill on a dusted cornstarch board and, with an anger tool or a round toothpick, ruffle both edges. *See figure 2.* Cut the frill in half. *See figure 3.*

Step 3. With a #2 tip, pipe royal icing along the cut edge of the frill. *See figure 4.* Attach to the base of the cake. Continue applying the sections until the lower ruffle is completed.

Step 4. Cut out the top ruffle and attach it to the cake *See figure 5* remembering to leave approximately a 1/2" (1.5 cm) space between the top and lower ruffle.

figure 1

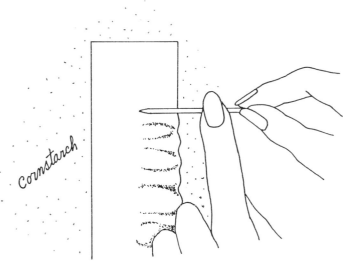

figure 2

figure 3

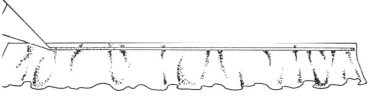

figure 4

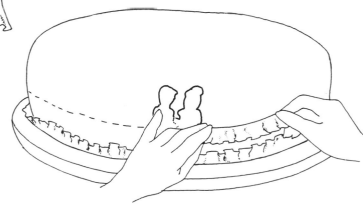

figure 5

Step 5. Repeat Step 2 for the 2nd ruffle from the base of the cake. Then, cut out the top ruffle, leaving the scallop attached. Ruffle the lower edge and, with a fan tool, press the design into each scallop. *See figure 6.*

   Apply the top ruffle with royal icing. This time when seaming the pieces together, pipe a small section of icing down the centre of both seams and smoothen with a palette knife or smooth-edged tool. Continue attaching the ruffle until the cake is completed. With a #2 tip, pipe a small bead border around the base of the cake and let dry. *See figure 7.*

Step 6. Attach ribbon around cakes. With a #0 tip, pipe the embroidery patterns on the cakes. Let dry. Place the ribbons around the cake boards.

Step 7. For confetti, roll out different shades of tiny hearts with gum paste and place at random over the front of the cake.

Embellishments

Peach roses
White Cattleya orchids
Pearls
White lace
Posy holders
Ribbon

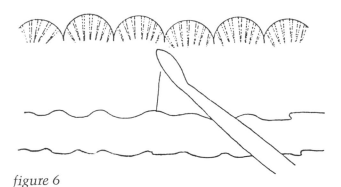

figure 6

figure 7

Chapter 8

Show Cakes

The excitement, the creative surge, the challenge of new ideas, the beautiful flowers and the thrill of winning—these are the joys I associate with my show cakes. Cake decorating shows are very special, exciting events. Here are a few tips to help you win.

First and foremost, read the guidelines *very* carefully for the category in which you wish to enter your cake. Follow these guidelines to the letter. (If the rules specify a 3-Tier Cake, then that is what you must make. If they state "no ribbon, just wire," then don't use ribbon.) If your cake does not match the guidelines exactly, the judges will disqualify you. Never enter a cake that has competed in another show. And finally, keep your work clean and simple and use monotone colours.

Now, go ahead and create your masterpiece. Looking forward to meeting you on the show floor.

Silver Anniversary Show Cake

Single Tier Round Filigree

Silver Medallist, Special Occasion Cakes, Escoffier Society Professional Section, Culinary Salon, Toronto 1987.

Step 1. Cover the board with fondant following instructions on page 91 and let dry overnight. Cover the cake with fondant and place on board. With a #2 tip, pipe a small bead border around the base of the cake and let dry at least 2 hours.

Step 2. Make a false collar and place it around the cake making sure the collar is resting on the bead border. *See figure 1.* Remove the collar and keep folding the collar to fit the pattern—allowing ¼" space between filigree pieces.

Step 3. Once the filigree pattern fits the false collar, tape the ends of the pattern over a soft drink can or glass. *See figure 2.* Then place a small sheet of cooking film over the pattern.

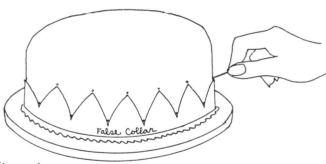

figure 1

figure 2

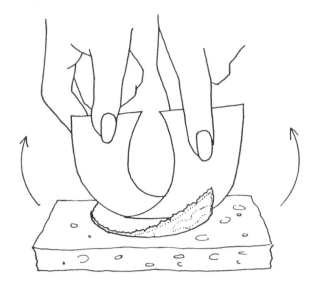

figure 3

Step 4. With a #0 tip, pipe the filigree pattern and leave to dry on the tin for at least 30 minutes. When dry, remove the pattern from the soft drink can and place very gently upside down on a sheet of foam. Carefully peel off the cooking film. *See figure 3.*

Step 5. With a #0 tip, pipe 3 dots on the reverse filigree pattern (one at the point and one each on the lower heart). *See figure 4.* Very gently attach all filigree pieces to the cake, overpiping with another dot on the previous dots. *See figure 5.* Let dry.

Step 6. Mix a small amount of edible silver colour with white alcohol. With a #1 fine paint brush, paint the outer pattern with silver colour.
Position the stencils on top of the cake and, with a palette knife, spread the stencils with royal icing. Let dry. When dry, paint with silver colour.

Embellishments

Calla lily
Leaves
Filigree (See pattern illustration)

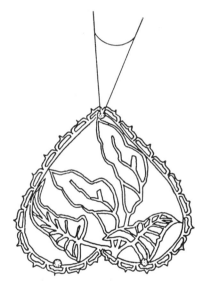

figure 4

figure 5

Filigree pattern

Ivory Bells Show Cake

2-Tier Flat Bell-Shaped

Gold Medallist, Escoffier Society Professional Section, Culinary Salon, Toronto 1987.

Many advanced cake decorating techniques are used in this unusual wedding cake—filigree bells; colour flow bride and groom; piped birds; pastillage book and rings and hollow layered string work.

Step 1. Cover the boards with fondant following instructions on page 91 and let dry overnight. Cover the cakes with fondant and place on the boards. With a #2 tip, pipe a small bead border around the base of the cakes and let dry overnight.

Step 2. Make a false collar and place around the cake. Mark the pattern on the sides of the cakes. *See figure 1.*

Step 3. With a #2 tip, pipe the lower scallop bridging for 6 lines (first line all the way around), 2nd, 3rd, 4th and 5th lines graduate ⅛″ (3 mm) from both ends, allowing each line to dry before attempting the next line. The 6th line must go all the way around. *See figure 2.* Let dry. With colour flow to the count of 10, colour flow the bridging. This both strengthens and hides the bridge work. Let dry 4 hours.

Step 4. With a #0 tip, pipe the strings down from the lower line to the bridge. *See figure 3.* Let dry. To make the upper hollow string work, first pipe a single scallop with a #2 tip onto a sheet of cooking film. *See figure 4.* (It is a good idea to pipe more than required.) Let dry. Remove one scallop at a time and with a #2 tip, attach each scallop to the cake. *See figure 5.* The hollow bridge is thus created. Let dry at least 2 hours.

Step 5. With a #0 tip, pipe the strings from the top pattern mark onto the hollow scallop. (Care must be taken with the piping or the hollow bridge line will break.) *See figure 6.* Let dry.

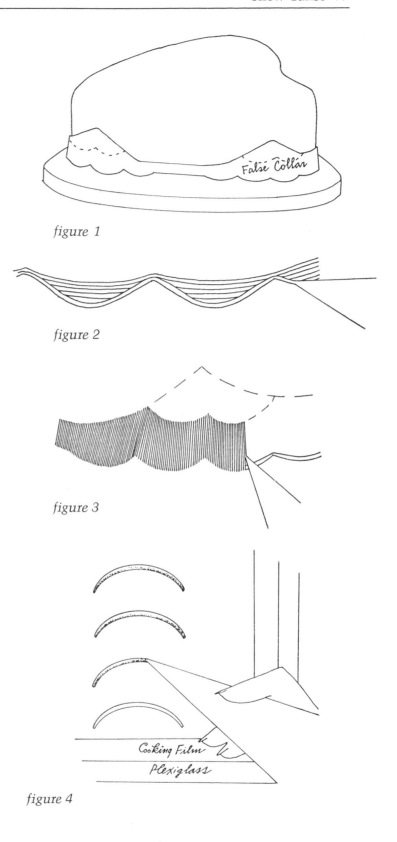

figure 1

figure 2

figure 3

figure 4

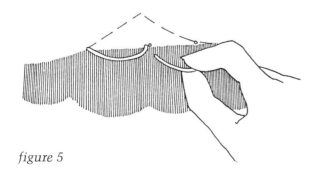

figure 5

figure 6

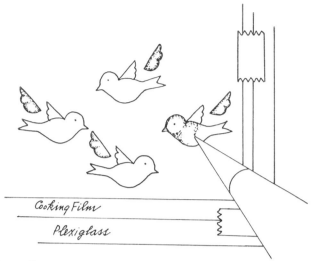

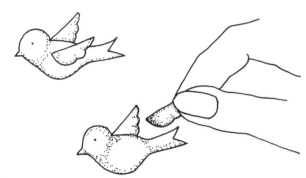

figure 7

figure 8

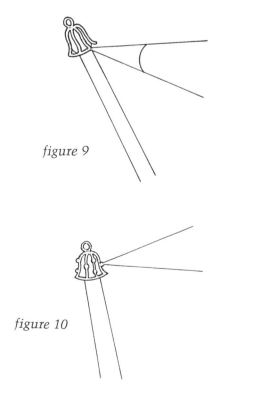

figure 9

figure 10

Step 6. With a #0 tip, pipe the lace pieces. Let dry. Pipe the small embroidery birds making the front wings first. *See figure 7.* Let dry. Using water, very slightly thin the royal icing and pipe the back wings and bodies of the birds, and, while it is still soft, attach the front wings. *See figure 8.* Let dry.

Step 7. Place some fondant inside the small, metal hollow bells, and attach onto an anger tool (this will help you turn the bells while piping them). Grease the outside of the bells with a small amount of white fat and, with a #0 tip, pipe a fine line down each bell. *See figure 9.* Pipe a solid line around the base of the bells to connect all the lines together. Pipe a small dot between the lines to strengthen them. *See figure 10.* Let dry. Pipe a small handle on top of the bells (turn bells upside down to do this) to attach to the cake.

Step 8. To remove the bells, hold each one over a low heat (i.e. the heating plate on the stove), and as the fat melts, the bell will slide off the mold. Set aside. To make the larger half-bells, repeat as above but this time pipe only a half-bell onto a large mold. Let dry and gently remove.

Step 9. To make the bride and groom, thin the royal icing with water so that it does not peak. With a #1 tip, first pipe the faces leaving the tip in the icing when piping. Allow the faces to crust over. While the faces are crusting over, pipe the main trouser leg and the bodice on the bride's dress. Repeat piping the pieces as numbers show. *See figure 11.* Make small forget-me-nots and attach to the bride's hair and bouquet. Roll out very thin strips of gum paste to make the bow on the bride's dress. Let dry 24 hours or longer.

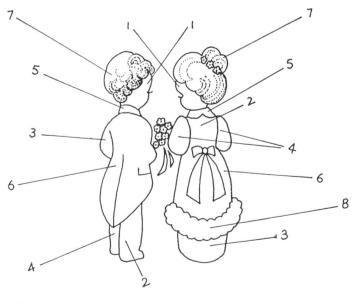

figure 11

Step 10. With a #1 tip, pipe a series of small hooks onto a sheet of cooking film. Let dry. When dry, attach the hooks to the hollow bridge work with a small amount of icing. *See figure 12.* Let dry.

Step 11. To assemble the cake, very gently lift the handle of each bell over the hook. With a small amount of royal icing, attach the bride and groom. For the confetti, roll out different shades of tiny hearts with gum paste and place at random over the front of the cake. With a #0 tip, pipe the embroidery and attach the birds. With a #0 tip, pipe a small scallop around the base of both strings. *See figure 13.*

Step 12. To make the books, roll out pastillage and cut desired size. Crimp the edges and set aside. Roll out the centre of the book, score the edges and attach the inside of the cover. Set aside to dry overnight. Set pastillage rings on book using a very fine line of royal icing.

Embellishments

Roses
Moth orchids
Ivy leaves
3 candles
Pastillage book with rings
Embroidery (See pattern illustration)

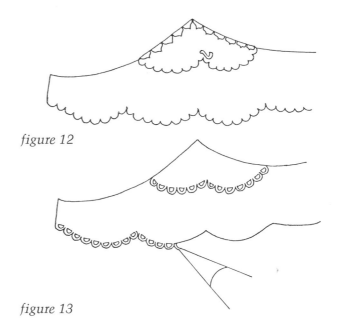

figure 12

figure 13

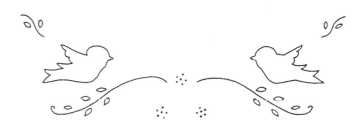

Embroidery pattern

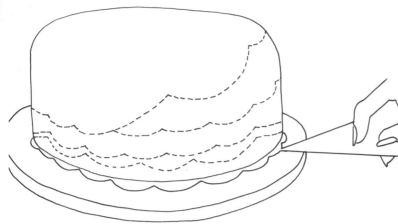

figure 1

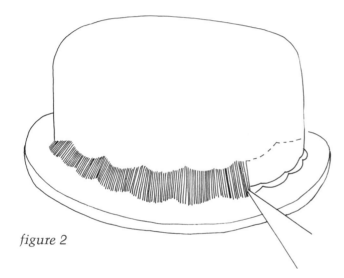

figure 2

Simply Elegant Show Cake

3-Tier Round

Silver Medallist, Wedding Cake Section, Toronto Bakers' Showcase, October 1988.

The most elegant of elegant cakes!

Step 1. Cover the boards with fondant following instructions on page 91 and let dry overnight. Cover the cakes with fondant following instructions on page 92 and place on the boards. Pipe a small bead border around the base of each cake. Let dry at least 1 hour.

Step 2. With a false collar, mark the pattern onto the side of the cakes using a pin or dressmaker's wheel. Remove the collar and with a #2 tip, pipe the bridging on the lower pattern only. *See figure 1.* Let dry. Flood in the bridge with pink icing taking care not to overfill the bridge. Let dry. With a #0 tip, pipe the strings from the lower pattern mark to the bridge. Let dry. *See figure 2.* Then pipe the 3 lines of scallops.

Step 3. With a #2 tip, repeat piping the next bridging, allowing it to dry before flooding in the bridge. Let dry. With a #0 tip, pipe the strings from the next marked pattern line to the bridge. Let dry.

Step 4. Repeat again piping the bridge. Let dry. Flood in and let dry. Pipe the 3rd pattern of strings. Let dry. Again, pipe the 3 rows of scallops. Let dry.

Step 5. Repeat again piping the final bridge at the top of the cake. Let dry. Flood in and let dry. With a cloth under the board to raise the cake, pipe the strings from the marked pattern line to the bridge. *See figure 3.* (This line of strings is very difficult to pipe as the strings want to fall on the top edge of the cake.) Let dry.

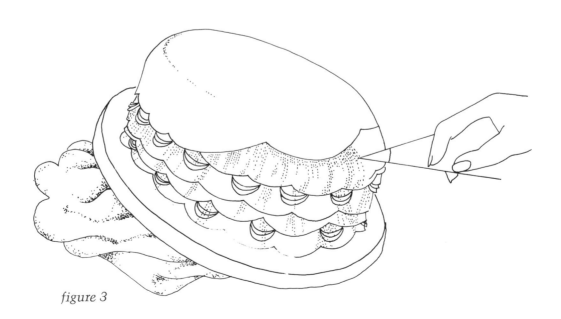

figure 3

Step 6. With a #0 tip, pipe the small scallops on top of the final strings. Remove the cloth from under the board. *See figure 4.*

Step 7. With a #0 tip, pipe the small scallop around all the bridging. *See figure 5.* When dry, very carefully turn the cake upside down and stand the cake on a large tin or glass jar. Continue piping the small scallops all around the top edge of the cake. *See figure 6.* Let dry. Very gently turn the cake right side up.

Step 8. With a #0 tip, pipe the embroidery around the sides of the cake. Let dry. Repeat for the other 2 tiers. Then attach ribbon to the sides of the boards. Place flowers on top of the cakes.

Embellishments

Roses
Sweet peas
Small lady slippers
Sprays of small pink forget-me-nots
Ivy leaves
Embroidery (See pattern illustration)

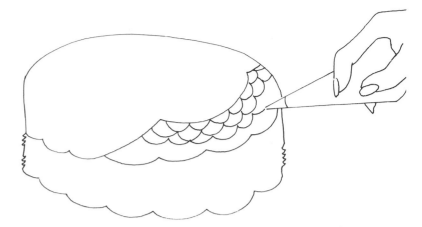

figure 4

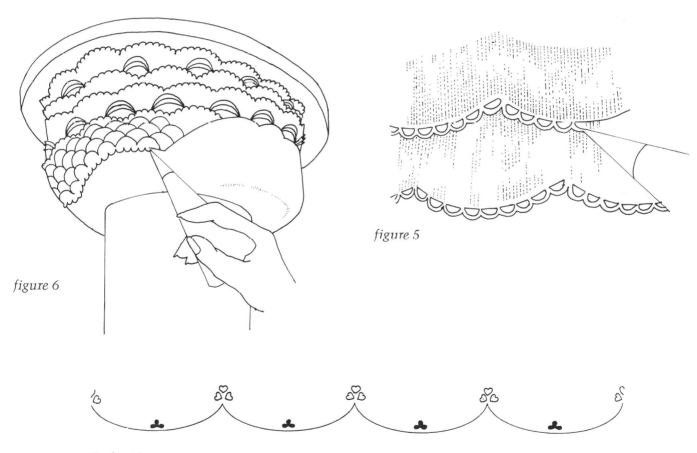

figure 6

figure 5

Embroidery pattern

Chapter 9

Recipes and Methods

RECIPES FOR CAKES

Many people have their own favourite recipes for cakes. Here are three that I have found work very well with fondant icing.

Fruit Cake

8″ (20.3 cm) round cake

Ingredients

Mixed dried fruit i.e. raisins,
sultanas and/or dates 2¹/₂lbs (1.2 kg)
Nuts (pecans and/or almonds) 6 ozs (200 g)
Mixed peel 4 ozs (125 g)
Glace cherries 6 ozs (200 g)
Sweet butter 10 ozs (300 g)
Brown sugar 10 ozs (300 g)
Eggs (large) 7
All purpose flour (Self-raising flour) 12 ozs (350 g)
Salt ¹/₄ level tsp (.65 ml)
Mixed spices 2 level tsp (1¹/₄ ml)
Brandy (optional) 3 Tbsp (45 ml)
Orange (both juice and rind) 1
Lemon (both juice and rind) 1

Method

Wash all the fruit and cherries and let dry for 2 days.
Line the cake tin with several layers of brown paper, with the final layer being either a wax paper or a greaseproof paper.

Cream the butter and sugar together very well.
Beat in the eggs one at a time.
Sieve the dry ingredients together and mix one cup of the dry ingredients into the mixture of fruit, nuts and grated rind.
Add gradually to the creamed mixture, with a little of the lemon and orange juices.
Finally, mix in the brandy.
Pour the mixture into the prepared cake tin and smooth the top of the cake with dampened fingers.

Bake in a slow oven 275°F (140°C) for approximately 4-5 hours.
When cold, remove from tin and re-wrap until cake is required.

Almond Cake

12″ (30.5 cm) round cake

Ingredients

Cooking almond paste (marzipan) 2 lbs (1 kg)
White sugar 1 lb (500 g)
Eggs (large) 12
Cake & Pastry Flour (All purpose flour) 8 ozs (250 g)
Apricot brandy (optional) 3 Tbsp (45 ml)
Prepare the cake tin as for the fruit cake.

Method

Cut the almond paste into small pieces and place in a mixer.
Add brandy and sugar and beat very well together.
Gradually add the eggs and beat at low speed for 10-15 mins until very smooth.
Finally, fold in the flour very gently.

Pour the mixture into the tin and bake at 350°F (175°C) for approximately 2-2¹/₂ hours.

This cake will keep fresh for up to a week, and can be served with fresh fruit, fresh whipping cream or ice cream.

Chocolate Chip Carrot Cake

My own recipe, guaranteed to please lovers of both chocolate and carrot cakes. This one I created when the bride wanted carrot cake and the groom asked for chocolate. It proved to be a delicious compromise!

8″ (20.3 cm) round cake.

Ingredients

Brown sugar 10 ozs (300 g)
Oil 10 ozs (325 ml)
Vanilla extract 1 tsp (5 ml)
Orange juice and rind 1
Baking powder 2 tsp (10 ml)
Baking soda 1 tsp (5 ml)
Salt 1 tsp (5 ml)
Carrots 1 lb (500 g)
Golden raisins 8 ozs (250 g)
Cinnamon 2 tsp (10 ml)
Nutmeg 1 tsp (5 ml)
Pecan pieces 8 ozs (250 g)
Large chocolate chips (semi-sweet) 12 ozs (375 g)
Large eggs 4
Flour (sifted) 12 ozs (375 g)

IVORY AND PEARLS RUFFLE CAKE

SILVER ANNIVERSARY SHOW CAKE

IVORY BELLS SHOW CAKE

SIMPLY ELEGANT SHOW CAKE

Prepare the cake tin as for the fruit cake.

Method

Prepare the carrots by peeling and finely processing through a blender. Set aside to add last to the batter. Sift the dry ingredients together and set aside. Combine the pecan pieces, raisins and chocolate chips and set aside.

Beat the sugar and oil together for 5 minutes. Add the extract, orange juice and peel. At medium speed, beat in the eggs, one at a time.

At low speed, add dry ingredients, then carrots, raisins, nuts and chocolate chips. Mix together slowly.

Pour batter into prepared tin and bake at 350°F (175°C) for approximately 1 hour.

This cake covers well with either marzipan or cream cheese frosting, then fondant (sugar paste).

Champagne Wedding Truffles

Many brides like to give out wedding favours. What could be more appropriate than a single wedding truffle!

Ingredients

White chocolate 1¹/₂ lbs (750 g)
Whipping cream 8 ozs (250 ml)
Cocoa butter 2 ozs (50 g)
Champagne 4 ozs (125 ml)
Extra white chocolate for coating 1 lb (500 g)

Method

Melt 1¹/₂ lbs of the white chocolate with the cocoa butter. Bring the whipping cream to a full rolling boil. Combine the melted chocolate to the whipping cream and stir. Let it cool slightly, then add the champagne. Set aside to thicken, stirring occasionally.

When thick, place in a mixing bowl and whip. Place in a piping bag and pipe small drops onto a parchment sheet. Let set. Dust hands with icing sugar (powdered sugar) and roll 2 truffles into balls. Dip in chocolate and set aside to harden. Dip again in chocolate and set aside. When ready, place in paper cups and serve.

RECIPES FOR ICING

Royal Icing

Many people feel that I have a secret for my string work. I have found that the best royal icing to use is made with egg whites, not meringue powder. Meringue powder royal icing does not have the strength or the stretch of egg white royal icing.

Ingredients

Egg white (medium) 1
Icing sugar (sifted) 8-10 ozs (225-300 g)
Gum arabic (for strength) ¹/₈ tsp (.65 ml)
Liquid glucose (for stretch) ¹/₄ tsp (1.25 ml)

Place the egg white in a glass bowl. Slowly add the sifted icing sugar (teaspoon by teaspoon) while mixing the icing with a knife.

Continue mixing until the icing is a soft peak, then add the sifted gum arabic, mix well.

Continue beating until a stiff peak is reached, then add the glucose and mix well.

Take the knife out of the bowl, cover the bowl with plastic wrap, then a damp cloth.

This icing will keep up to 3 days for string work, although it must be freshly stirred each morning. You may also have to add a small amount of extra sifted icing sugar.

Note: For Filigree work, use the above recipe but *omit* the liquid glucose.

Fondant Icing (Plastic or Sugar Paste)

Ingredients

Gelatin 1 pkg (15 ml)
Cold water ¹/₄ cup (60 ml)

Mix the above together, let stand 5 minutes, then melt over a saucepan of hot water over a gentle heat until completely dissolved. *Do not overheat.*

Icing sugar 2 lbs (900 g)

Sift the icing sugar into a bowl, making a well in the centre of the icing sugar.

Glucose ¹/₂ cup (125 ml)
Glycerine (optional) 1 Tbsp (15 ml)

Add the above ingredients to the heated gelatin, stirring well until smooth.

Pour the mixture into the icing sugar.

With a spoon, stir the icing sugar from the sides of the bowl into the mixture.

When stiff, turn the mixture onto the counter and knead in the remainder of the sugar. Wrap in a plastic wrap, and let rest for 2 hours before using.

Chocolate Fondant Icing (Plastic or Sugar Paste)

Ingredients

Gelatin 1 pkg (15 ml)
Cold water ¹/₄ cup (60 ml)
Icing sugar 2 lbs (1 kg)
Cocoa powder (Pure, unsweetened) 4 ozs (125 g)
Glucose 4 ozs (125 g)
Cooking oil 2 ozs (60 ml)
Glycerine (optional) 1 Tbsp (15 ml)

Method

Mix the gelatin and the cold water together. Let stand 5 minutes then melt mixture over a saucepan of hot water over a gentle heat until completely dissolved. (Do not overheat.)
Sift the icing sugar and cocoa into a bowl, making a well in the centre of the icing sugar.
Add the glucose, cooking oil and glycerine to the heated gelatin, stirring well until mixture is smooth. Pour the mixture into the icing sugar.
With a spoon, stir the icing sugar from the sides of the bowl into the mixture.
When stiff, turn the mixture onto the counter and knead in the remainder of the sugar. Wrap in plastic wrap and let rest 15 minutes before using.

Pastillage

There are many different recipes for pastillage. The one I used for both the music cards and boxes is very simple.

Sift 1 tsp (5 ml) of gum tragacanth and ¹/₂tsp (2.5 ml) of gum arabic into 1 cup (250 ml) of royal icing. Work in extra sifted icing sugar until pliable. Wrap well in plastic wrap until ready to use. When drying any pieces of pastillage, it is always best to keep turning the pieces over to allow for even drying.

Covering a Cake Board

Step 1: Brush the cake board with clear piping gel. *See figure 1.*
Step 2: Place the board on a small container to elevate. *See figure 2.*
Step 3: Dust the counter top with a small amount of cornstarch and roll out the fondant. *See figure 3.* When large enough to cover the board, gently lift the fondant onto the board and roll the rolling pin over the fondant to release the air. *See figure 4.*
Step 4: Trim the excess fondant from the side of the board. *See figure 5.*
Step 5: Set aside and always let dry overnight before placing the cake on the board.

figure 1

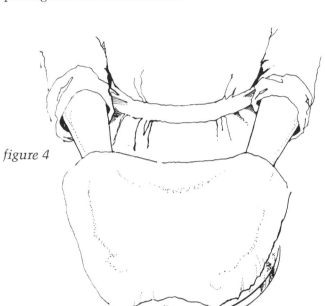

figure 4

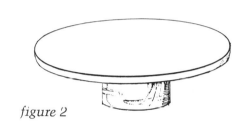

figure 2

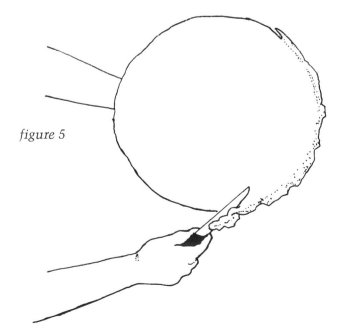

figure 5

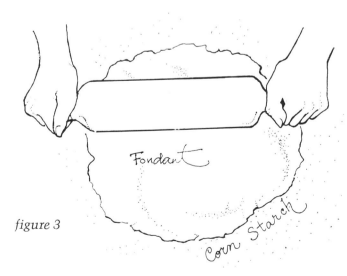

figure 3

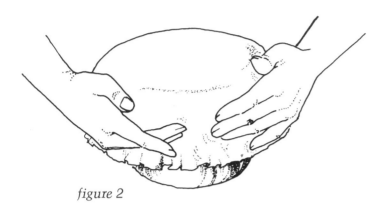

figure 1

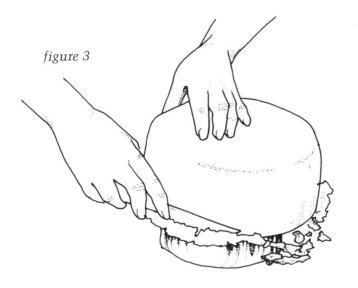

figure 2

Covering a Cake

It is always much easier to cover a cake if the cake is elevated on a stand with a smaller radius than the cake.

If you are covering a styrofoam dummy first, sand the top edges of the form to create a softer look. Brush the dummy cake with piping gel (or boiled and sifted apricot jam, or vodka) if you are using a real cake. *See figure 1.* Set aside on the dummy.

For rolling out the fondant, use either a lightly oiled large plastic sheet, or first dust the counter with a small amount of cornstarch. Lightly oil the rolling pin. When the fondant has been rolled out large enough to cover the cake, gently slide both hands underneath the fondant and carefully place it on the cake. Roll the top of the cake with the rolling pin to release any air, and with the sides of your hands, gently lift and smooth the sides. *See figure 2.* Trim the bottom edge of the cake by placing a knife against the bottom of the cake to trim off the excess fondant. *See figure 3.* Carefully lift and place the cake in the centre of the board. If crimper work is required, it must be done immediately before the fondant dries.

To mark the cake with a pattern, use adding machine tape 1¹/₄″ (3.5 cm) wide to make a false collar. Tape the two edges together, *See figure 4*, and gently slide the collar off the cake. Keep folding the collar in half until the desired size of scallops is

figure 3

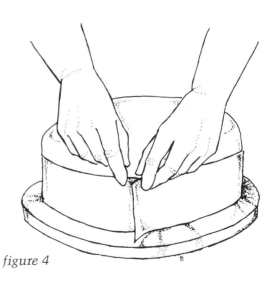

figure 4

attained. *See figure 5.* Place the collar back on the cake and with a small pin, mark the high point of the scallop. *See figure 6.* With a small dressmaker's wheel, roll the wheel around the top of the collar. *See figure 7.*

Remove the false collar to reveal cake now marked with pattern for placement of royal icing. Make up a parchment bag. *See figure 8.* With a #2 tip, pipe a small bead border around the base of the cake. Let dry. *See figure 9.* With the #2 tip, pipe a line of scallops all around the cake. *See figure 10.*

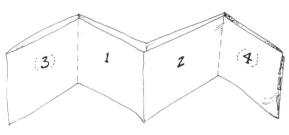

figure 5

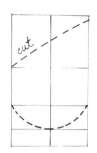

figure 6

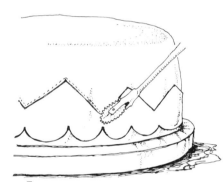

figure 7

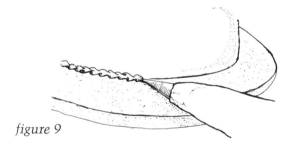

figure 9

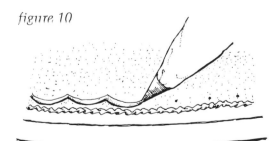

figure 10

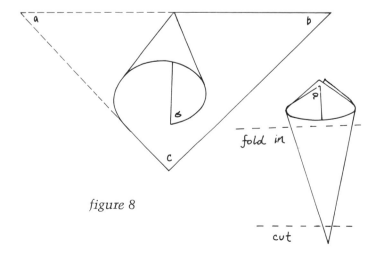

figure 8

The second row should start approximately ¼″ (7 mm) from the end. Repeat for the 3rd, 4th and 5th rows starting and ending within the shorter distance. *See figure 11.* Let dry. The 6th row must be piped all the way around the length of the first scallop. (This solid line will help strengthen the bridge.) Let dry. Mix up flood-in icing to the count of 10, (you can add colour if required) and flood-in the bridge work. (This will add both colour and strength to the bridge.) With a #0 tip, pipe strings from the top marked line down to the bridge. Let dry. *See figure 12.* With a #0 tip, pipe the lace pieces onto a small sheet of wax paper. Let dry. *See figure 13.* To attach the lace pieces to the cake, pipe 4 small dots onto the top of the strings, and very gently attach the lace pieces to the dots. (Always attach the lace pieces at a slight angle, as it creates a much softer look.) *See figure 14.* To finish the cake, cover its side(s) with a ribbon, attaching ribbon with a small pin. *See figure 15.*

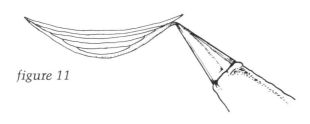

figure 11

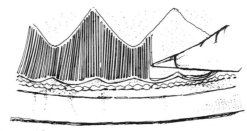

figure 12

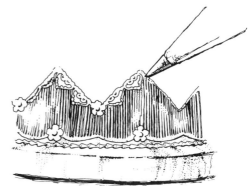

figure 14

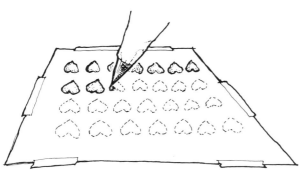

figure 13

figure 15

Dowelling a Cake

All tiered cakes should be dowelled to prevent any accidents. Soft cakes can slip in warm weather or sink into the cake they are sitting on. Most dowels are made from ¼" (7 mm) wood, or, for heavy liquor type cakes, a ½" (13 mm) dowel.

First, with a template, mark on the tops of the cakes where you are going to place the pillars. *See figure 1.* Remove the template and with a meat skewer or long needle, push the needle down into the base of the cake. Remove the needle and replace it with the wooden dowel. *See figure 2.* Many Australian style cakes are better supported when the dowels go into the cake and through the hollow pillar, *See figure 3*, although the dowel can be cut off at the top of the cake. Attach the pillars with royal icing and set the top tier on the pillars.

figure 1

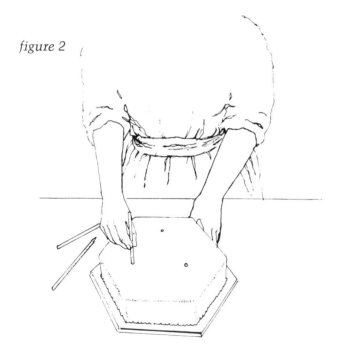

figure 2

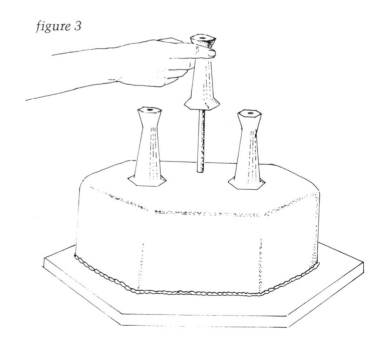

figure 3

Flood-Work

Colour flow is also known as flow in, run sugar or flood in.

Before starting any type of run-in work, it is always best to make the icing the day before to help eliminate any air bubbles in the mixture. Always mix the pre-made icing in a glass bowl, stirring slowly with a knife and adding a small amount of water until the desired count is reached. (Count refers to the number of seconds required for icing cut with the flat side of a knife to rejoin with no marks or impressions.)

Draw pattern on a sheet of tracing paper, and place the paper on a plexiglass (or glass) square. Cover the paper with either cooking film or thin plastic wrap and tape it down. Outline the pattern with a #1 or #2 tip and, with the run-in icing, flood the pattern outlined. When working on collars, it is necessary to rotate the work so that both sides are worked on simultaneously. (Do not start at one side and work around to the other side, as the first section completed will start to dry and a line will show, as dry run cannot be blended with wet run in. Tap the work lightly on the table and place in the oven at 200°F (100°C) for 15 minutes, leaving the oven door open and the oven turned off. This allows the work to crust over. Leave the run-in work for approximately 48 hours before using.

Stencilling

Stencils are a very fast and effective method of cake decorating.

There are many kinds of commercial stencils available—plastic, coated cardboard, silk screens (for use with air brushing) and stainless steel. They are easily made at home, too, using an electric stencil-cutting pen and sheets of acetate or mylar.

To decorate with stencils, first, place the stencil(s) on the cake. (If the cake is iced with a butter cream frosting, let the frosting crust over before trying to stencil.) With a small palette knife, spread either royal icing, butter cream or melted chocolate over the stencil. By drawing the side of a clean palette knife over the stencil, carefully remove the excess frosting. Gently remove the stencil. Repeat until all stencils are placed on the cake.

Stencils can also be air brushed onto cakes.